HEAVEN AND HELL

in Buddhist Perspective

HEAVEN AND HELL

in Buddhist Perspective

by

B. C. LAW

PILGRIMS PUBLISHING
◆Varanasi◆

HEAVEN AND HELL IN BUDDHIST PERSPECTIVE

B C LAW

Published by:
PILGRIMS PUBLISHING

An imprint of:
PILGRIMS BOOK HOUSE
(Distributors in India)
B 27/98 A-8, Nawabganj Road
Durga Kund, Varanasi-221010, India
Tel: 91-542-2314060 Fax: 91-542-2312456
E-mail: pilgrims@satyam.net.in
Website: www.pilgrimsbooks.com

PILGRIMS BOOK HOUSE (New Delhi)
9 Netaji Subhash Marg, 2nd Floor
Daryaganj, New Delhi 110002
Tel: 91-11-23285081
E-mail: pilgrim@del2.vsnl.net.in

First Published in 1925

Cover design by Sasya

ISBN: 81-7769-085-X

Printed in India at Pilgrim Press Pvt. Ltd. Lalpur Varanasi

INTRODUCTION TO THE NEW EDITION

The perception of the human mind to the existence of an after-world with an equally puzzling after-life has led to the creation of a space equally occupying time, where the spirit is rewarded or punished for its earthly actions. This co-consequential existence, both terrifying and awesome, has been used as a tool by religions from time immemorial in order to coerce a person to maintain a dignified and pure existence. Dante's heaven and hell depicting both the fiery abyss and the perfection of purity is not that much different from similar concepts put forward by other religious groups.

The Buddhist approach on the other hand provides us with a novel concept seeing only the inherent good in any erring spirit and condemning such souls to a temporary purgatory from where they may emerge purified and whole. B C Law using his immense knowledge of the subject and ample Pali literature to present and elaborately describe the varying degrees of purgatory as perceived by the Buddhist mind, has clearly defined these states, thus cataloguing the different aspects in relation to their Karma and their deserts as they pass on to the next plane of existence.

The varying pleasures of the heavens and turmoil of the hells, we are told, are equally impermanent and only a transitory stage in the onward journey of the soul as it moves from life to life and eventually to *nirvana* from whence it becomes at one with the whole never more to wander aimlessly on through the travails of this worldly existence of pain and agony. This book clearly and lucidly exposes the Buddhist view of the after-world and life, thereby clarifying any misconceptions the reader may have had about what may appear as a godless faith having no real aspiration to what other religions describe as a spiritual state.

B C Law has written several other books related to this subject, which introduce us to the Buddhist concept of the after-life—the existence of a space in time related to the greater conception of the creation. Buddha's whole approach to the question of life and death fully incorporated the Hindu ideals of re-incarnation and their feelings towards karma, this being the result of one's own actions in the present life. He has allowed us the benefit of the opportunity through our own good offices, to improve upon our lot in the future plan of things.

Christopher N Burchett
June 2003
Varanasi.

FOREWORD

With the publication of the following pages Dr. Bimala Charan Law adds yet another volume to the series of interesting studies of Buddhism, upon which he has for some years past been engaged. In his "Kṣatriya Clans in Buddhist India" and in his larger and more detailed treatment of the same subject entitled "Some Kṣatriya Tribes of Ancient India", he gave us an interesting historical account of the peoples and politics of the Ganges Valley at the time of Buddha. In his "Life and Work of Buddhaghosa" he presented us with a portrait of the great Buddhist commentator of the fifth century A. D., and a little later he published a small volume on "The Buddhist Conception of Spirits." The present volume is written on much the same lines as this latter treatise and forms a useful companion volume to it. In it Dr. Law sets before the reader the Buddhist idea of Heaven and Hell, or, perhaps it would be more correct to say, the ideas of Heaven and Hell prevalent amongst the people of northern India at the time of Buddha and incorporated subsequently in the Buddhist scriptures. For it is clear from the comparison which Dr. Law draws between the Buddhist and Brahmanical ideas of Hell that they are derived from the same source. Moreover there is a good deal concerning the various Heavens and Hells of which Dr. Law tells us, that is quite obviously foreign to the lofty thought and teaching of Buddha himself. The joys of Heaven are represented as being obtainable by means of what is suspiciously like a mercenary bargain, entered into in a spirit which far from being selfless is, on the contrary, frankly selfish. One example taken from a number given by Dr. Law will suffice to make this clear. The daughter of a family of Rājagaha on learning that the act of giving is like the tree which fulfils every wish, at once becomes eager to practise charity. An opportunity presents itself with the appearance upon the scene of a Buddhist monk, to whom she offers a seat and food. While thus practising the virtue of charity, she prays that in return she may receive after death as a fitting reward for her piety, a whole host of heavenly gifts, including a celestial elephant. Her prayer is granted and she passes at death into the Tāvatiṁsa Heaven where she dwells in a golden mansion with a retinue of a thousand heavenly maidens, and receives amongst other things the coveted elephant. Not in this way, it need hardly be pointed out, is Nirvāṇa, the *Summum bonum* which the Lord Buddha held out to suffering humanity, to be attained. Indeed, piety practised in this calculating spirit, far from bringing

Nirvāṇa within reach of man, could serve only to bind him more securely to the wheel of life. Dr. Law himself sums up the position concisely when he writes—"The highest of the pleasures that these Heavens bestow has a limit......They can never bring about a final release from evil and hence, the experiences in Heaven, though pleasurable, are an evil to be guarded against—the more so on account of their luring attractiveness."

But it is only in the mind of the non-Indian readers that any confusion between Nirvāṇa and Heaven is likely to arise. And in his case this volume will serve to dispel any confusion that may exist. For it is made abundantly clear that the Heavens and Hells of Buddhism are places within the categories of space and time, whose inhabitants, whether gods or devils, are as much subject to the iron law of *karma* as are the dwellers upon this earth itself. In a sense the Heavens and Hells, of which we read in these pages, may be said to exist for the purpose of providing a more elaborate stage than this earth can do, for the play of the ever revolving cycle of existence and all that it involves. The various heavens make possible greater and more varied reward in the case of those who by meritorious lives, have earned it ; the different hells greater and more varied measures of retribution. Dr. Law has been at pains to collect from Buddhist literature a number of descriptions both of the pleasures of Heaven and of the sorrows of Hell. These are interesting as showing the nature of the rewards and punishments which in those early days, were considered appropriate to particular acts of piety and particular sins. The catalogue of crimes and their corresponding punishments, for example, is given in elaborate detail. And if the reader after perusal of the volume has not acquired a comprehensive knowledge of the eschatology of popular Buddhism, he will have no one but himself to blame, for Dr. Law has admirably accomplished the task which he set out to perform.

November, 1924. Ronaldshay.

PREFACE

The present treatise is a thesis approved by the Calcutta University for Sir Asutosh Mookerjee gold medal, 1924. The Pāli literature is full of details regarding various Heavens and Hells recognised by the ancient Buddhists. The present volume furnishes us for the first time with an exhaustive and comparative treatment of the subject. I shall consider my labour amply rewarded if this little brochure is well received by the public.

I am glad to put in an appendix Dr. B. M. Barua's short note entitled "Books of Stories of Heaven and Hell" which will no doubt be very interesting to readers.

I am greatly indebted to the Right Hon'ble The Earl of Ronaldshay, P. C., G. C. S. I., G. C. I. E., D. Litt., D. L., etc., etc., Ex-Governor of Bengal, who takes great interest in my works, for his learned foreword to this volume.

Calcutta,
24, Sukea's Street,
April, *1925*.

BIMALA CHARAN LAW

CONTENTS

PART I —HEAVEN

SECTION I

Heavens as generally described in the Nikāyas 1

SECTION II

SECTION III

Observations 86

PART II —HELL 92

Index 127

APPENDIX

Books of Stories of Heaven and Hell
By Dr. B. M. Barua, M. A., D. Litt.

BIBLIOGRAPHY

1. Abhidhammattha Saṁgaha (Kosambī's Ed.)
2. Abhidharmakoṣavyākhyā
3. A catena of Buddhist Scriptures (Beal)
4. Aṅguttara Nikāya
5. Buddhism as a religion (Hackmann)
6. Buddhism, Primitive and Present (Copleston)
7. Buddhist Parables (Burlingame)
8. Buddhist Philosophy (Keith)
9. Catubhāṇavāra
10. Chinese Buddhism (Edkins)
11. Dhammapada commentary
12. Dialogues of the Buddha
13. Dīgha Nikāya
14. Encyclopædia of Religion and Ethics (Hastings)
15. Hinduism and Buddhism (Eliot)
16. Indian Buddhism (Kern)
17. J. P. T. S., 1884
18. Jaina Sūtras (S. B. E.)
19. Jātaka (Fausböll)
20. Kathāvatthu (P. T. S.)
21. Khuddakapāṭha commentary
22. Mahāvastu
23. Majjhima Nikāya
24. Manorathapuraṇī
25. Mārkaṇḍeya Purāṇa (Pargiter)

BIBLIOGRAPHY

26. Pāli Dictionary (Childers)
27. Pañcagatidīpanaṁ
28. Petavatthu
29. Petavatthu commentary
30. Psalms of the Brethren (Mrs. Rhys Davids)
31. Samyutta Nikāya
32. Some Kṣatriya Tribes of Ancient India (B. C. Law)
33. Sumangalavilāsinī (P. T. S.)
34. Sutta Nipāta (P. T. S.)
35. Sutta Nipāta (S. B. E.)
36. Systems of Buddhistic Thought (Yamakami Sogen)
37 Vibhaṅga
38. Vimānavatthu commentary (P. T. S.)
39. Visuddhimagga (P. T. S.)
40. Yamaka (P. T. S.)

PART I—HEAVEN

Heavens as generally described in the Nikāyas

The Pāli literature describes the various heavens and their respective positions, one above the other, and the gods that reside there progressing in power and refinement. The Dīgha Nikāya of the Sutta-Piṭaka refers to some of the heavens in the Kevaddha Sutta. There the Buddha relates to Kevaddha how a bhikkhu of his congregation was troubled in mind by a certain problem (*viz.* where are earth, water, fire and wind—the four great elements, completely destroyed ?). The bhikkhu practised such a samādhi (meditation) that the path leading to the world of gods became clear to him. First he went to the Cātummahārājika gods for the solution of the above problem. He was asked by them to go to the four Mahārājās of the Cātummahārājika heaven. He then went to them and put the same question, but was asked to go to the gods of the Tāvatiṁsa heaven, who sent him on to their King Sakka who sent him on to the Yāma gods who sent him on to their King Suyāma who sent him on to the Tusita gods who sent him on to their

Heavens in the Kevaddha Sutta.

King Santusita who sent him on to the Nimmānarati gods who sent him on to their King Sunimmita who sent him on to the Paranimmitavasavattī gods who sent him on to their King Vasavattī who advised him to go to the gods of the Brahma world. He had to practise such a meditation as would enable him to go to the Brahmaloka. He went to the gods of the Brahma world who sent him to Mahābrahmā who appeared before him. The bhikkhu put to him the question which even Mahābrahmā could not answer, and he was advised to go to the Buddha. At last the Buddha gave a satisfactory reply to his query (Dīgha Nikāya, Vol. I., pp. 211-223, Kevaddha Suttanta).

Seven regions of the gods : compared with the seven Vedic regions.

It is clear from the above account that there are seven regions of the gods specified—there is the Cātummahārājika heaven, next the Tāvatiṁsa heaven, next in order come the regions of the Yāma gods, the Tusita gods, the Nimmānarati gods and the Paranimmitavasavattī gods—the gods of these six heavens belong to the Kāmāvacaraloka (i.e. the world as sensed and subjectively the mental plane of sensuous experience). Next comes the Brahma world. With this we may compare the seven *lokas* or regions of the Vedic literature and we observe an agreement, though, at first sight, there seems to be a difference. The seven Vedic regions are Bhu, Bhuvaḥ, Svar, Maha, Jana, Tapas and Satya or the Brahmaloka. The twice four or eight great kings (Mahārājikas) are apparently the eight *Dikpālas*, the lords of the quarters, so that their regions make up nothing but the *Bhur-loka* with its ruling deities. The Bhuvar-loka of which Indra is the master has its counter-part in the Tāvatiṁsa heaven where Sakka, who is the same as Indra, dominates. The name *Tāvatiṁsa* or thirty-three is very significant as the Vedic gods are only thirty-three in number. The *Tapo-loka* is also called the *Satya-loka* or the *Brahma-loka* in Brahmanical literature. Thus the highest regions in the two systems are identical. In the Brahmajāla Sutta of the same Nikāya (Dialogues, II., p. 31) also we have a reference to Brahmā and his palace. The Tevijja Sutta of this Nikāya (Vol. I. pp. 236 foll) also speaks of the union of men with Brahmā, but there Brahmā appears to stand more for *Brahma* of the Brahmanical system than Brahmā, the Creator-God.

Ābhassaraloka.

The *World of Radiance* (Ābhassara loka) described in the Brahmajāla Suttanta is one of the higher *Brahmalokas*. The above Suttanta tells us that at the beginning of a new world system a being falls from the Ābhassara loka on account of loss of life or merit and he is reborn in the Brahmavimāna which is then empty and there he dwells with his mental body (monomaya), living in joy, having a lustrous body and moving in the sky. (Dīgha Nikāya, Vol. I, p. 17).

The palace of Brahmā.

The Buddha relates later on in the same Suttanta that this god who is first reborn in the Brahmavimāna, or the palace of Brahmā, is the Great Brahmā; he considers himself superior to the other Ābhassaradevas who are subsequently reborn in the same vimāna, and these latter also show him the same respect.

Two classes of gods-Khiddāpadosikā and Manopadosikā.

The Brahmajāla Suttanta also tells us of two classes of gods, the Khiḍḍāpadosikā and the Manopadosikā. Both these classes are of a rather low order. Thus the Blessed One says that the Khiḍḍāpadosikā gods spend their time in laughing, playing and enjoying sensual pleasures. For this reason they lose control over their mind, as a result of which they fall down from their situation and are reborn in the human world. (Dīgha Nikāya, Vol. I., pp. 19-20). Of the second class, *viz.*, the Manopadosikā gods, the Buddha says that they think much of one another. In consequence of excessive thinking, their mind becomes polluted and on account of pollution of their mind, they fall down from that situation and are reborn in the human world. (Ibid., p.20).

Classification of gods in the Aṅguttara Nikāya.

In the Aṅguttara Nikāya also we have a classification of the gods. It says that there are the Cātummahārājika gods, Tāvatiṁsa gods, Yāma gods, Tusita gods, Nimmānarati gods, Paranimmitavasavattins, Brahmakāyikas and also gods superior to them. (Aṅguttara Nikāya, Vol. 1., p. 210).

The Mahāsamaya Suttanta-gods of the earth.

In the Mahāsamaya Suttanta, the Buddha mentions some gods who are found on this earth and also in the regions above. There are gods of Kapilavatthu, gods of the Himālayas, gods of Sātāgira, gods of Vessāmitta, Kumbhīra of Rājagaha, Dhataraṭṭha, ruler of the east and his sons, each of whom was named Inda, Virū ha, king of the Kumbhaṇḍas ruling the south, his sons, each of whom was named Inda ; Virūpakka, king of the nāgas ruling in the south and his sons, each of whom was called Inda ; Kuvera, king of the Yakkhas, ruling the north and his sons, each of whom was called Inda ; servants of the four mahārājās, Māyā, Kuṭeṇḍu, Veṭeṇḍu, Viṭucca, Viṭuc, Candana, Kāmaseṭṭha, Kinnughaṇḍu, Nighaṇḍu, Panāda, Opamañña, Mātali, the charioteer of gods, the musician Cittasena, Ñala, Janesabha, Pañcasikha, Suriyavaccasā, the Nāgas from Vesālī with Tacchaka, Kambalas, Assataras and Pāyāgas with all their relatives, Yamunā, Dhataraṭṭha, Erāvana the mahānāga, Kālakañjas, Vepacitti, Sucitti, Pahārāda and Namucī, all the sons of Bali, each of whom was named Veroca, gods of water, earth, fire and air ;

Varunas, Soma with Yasa, gods of compassion and kindness, Veṇhu (Viṣṇu), Sahalī, Asamas, Yamas, moon with its followers, sun with its followers, Mandavalāhaka with stars, Vāsava, the chief of Vasus, Sahabhu, Ariṭṭhakas, Rojas, Varuṇas, Sahadhammas, Accutas, Anejakas, Suleyyas, Vāsavanesi deities, samaṇas, mahāsamaṇas, mānusas, Khiḍḍāpadosikās, Manopadosikās, Haraya, Lohitavāsīs, Pāragas, Mahāpāragas, Sukka, Aruṇa, Veghanasa, Odātagayha, Vicakkhana, Sadāmatta, Hāragaja, Missaka, Pajjunna, Khemiyas, Tusita and Yāma gods, Kaṭṭhakas, Lambītakas, Lāmaseṭṭhas, Joti, Āsava, Nimmānarati, Paranimmita, Tissa, Subrahmā, Sanaṁkumāra and Mahābrahmā. (Dīgha Nikāya, Vol. II, pp. 253 foll). In the Mahāvastu we find a reference to all these gods with the addition of Śīva. (cf. Mahāvastu, Edited by Senart, Vol. I., p. 245; Ibid, Vol. III., p. 68; Ibid, Vol. III., p. 77).

Various grades of gods in the Dhānañjāni Suttam.

The Dhānañjāni Suttam of the Majjhima Nikāya furnishes the following account of the various grades of the gods :—Cātummahārājikā, Tāvatiṁsā, Yāmā, Tusitā, Nimmānarati, Paranimmitavasavattī.

After these there is the Brahmaloka.

One can reach the Brahmaloka after meditating on mettā, karuṇā, muditā and upekkhā and after developing these to the extent of all the quarters. (Majjhiṁa Nikāya, Vol. II., pp. 194-195).

Gods in the Dhammacakkappavattana Sutta.

The Dhammacakkappavattana Sutta besides mentioning the lower gods, gives the designations of the various grades of gods who make up the Brahmaloka. After giving a list of the six grades of gods from the Bhummadevas, it thus goes on to the Brahmapārisajjā and other devas mentioned below:-

1. Bhummadevas *i.e.* gods living on earth such as rukkhadevas.

1. Cātummahārājikadevas *i.e.* gods who are subjects of four guardian angels of four quarters.

2. Tāvatiṁsadevas *i.e.* gods dwelling in the Tāvatiṁsa heaven.

3. Yāmadevas *i.e.* gods dwelling in Yāma heaven.

4. Tusitadevas.

5. Nimmānaratidevas.

6. Paranimmitavasavattidevas.

These are the six Kāmāvacaradevas in heaven.

	Brahmapārisajjā	Vehapphalā	Devas dwelling in Brahmaloka.
	Brahmapurohitā	Avihā	
	Mahābrahma	Atappā	
Ābhassara Brahmās	Parittābhā	Sudassā	
	Appamānābhā	Sudassī	
	Ābhassarā	Akaniṭṭhakā	
	Parittosubha		
	Āppamanasubhā		
	Subhakihnakā		

(Catubhāṇavāra, Sinhalese Edition, pp. 30-35).

Some special gods are referred to in the Anuruddha Suttam of the Majjhima Nikāya :—

Special gods of the Anuruddha Suttam.

1. One becomes a parittābhadeva if he dies after finishing meditation on a small circle of light (parittaṁ ālokakaṣiṇaṁ).

2. One becomes a appamānābhadeva if he dies after finishing meditation on a boundless circle of light (appamāna ālokakaṣiṇaṁ).

3. One becomes a Saṁkiliṭṭhābhadeva if he dies after finishing meditation on impure light.

4. One becomes a parisuddhābhadeva if he dies after finishing meditation on pure light. (Majjhima Nikāya, Vol. III., p. 147).

Gods of the Kāmaloka Rūpaloka and Arūpaloka.

The Majjhima Nikāya also in the Sāleyyaka Sutta gives a list of all the gods of the Kāmaloka, Rūpaloka and Arūpaloka in the proper order though without the details which, however, must have been known to the author of these Suttas. Those who are pious and restrained may be born in Cātummahārājika, Tāvatiṁsa, Yāma, Tusita, Nimmānarati, Paranimmitavasavattī, Bramakāyika and other heavens up to Nevasaññānāsaññāyatana. (Majjhima Nikāya, Vol. I., p. 289). The disciples of the Buddha who are greatly learned and Ariyasāvakas know Pajāpati, Brahmā, Ābhassara gods, Subhakiṇṇa gods, Vehapphala, Abhibhu, Ākāsānañcāyatana,

Viññāṇañcāyatana, Ākiñcaññāyatana, Nevasaññānāsaññāyatana gods. (Majjhima Nikāya, Vol. I., p. 2). The bhikkhus who are pious, faithful, greatly learned, charitable and wise, exert to be born in the Cātummahārājika heaven knowing that the lease of life there is very long. They are born in this heaven in consequence of their exertion. Similarly, they exert to be born in other devalokas commencing from the Tāvatiṁsa heaven to the Nevasaññānāsaññāyatana heaven, learning that the lease of life in these devalokas is very long and they are born in these devalokas in consequence of their exertion. (Majjhima Nikāya, Vol. III., pp. 100-103). Many of the Brahmakāyikadevas are also mentioned in the Brahmanimantaṇika Sutta of the same Nikāya. (Majjhima Nikāya, Vol. I., p. 329).

Devas and spirits in the Āṭānāṭiya Suttanta.

In the Āṭānāṭiya Suttanta of the Dīgha Nikāya we find King Vessavana Kuvera reciting the Rakkhāmanta of Āṭānāṭa. In the course of this Rakkhāmanta we find the names of several spirits and devas which are of importance. (Dīgha Nikāya, Vol. III., pp. 204-205).

The sun is called Aditi's child (Aditiyāputto) (Dialogues of the Buddha, pt. III., 190 fn). This is quite in agreement with the Vedic idea of the sun as one of the ādityas. It further mentions Dhataraṭṭha, the sovereign lord of the Gandhabbas (Dīgha Nikāya, Vol. III., p. 197), Virū ha, the

2

king of the Kumbhāṇḍa sprites, Virūpākkha, the king of the Nāgas and Kuvera, the king of the Yakkhas. Vessavana gives a list of some of the Yakkhas to whom an appeal should be made for protection against these creatures, Yakkhas, Gandhabbas, Kumbhāṇḍas and Nāgas, who, as he says, are not humane but are rough, irascible and violent. It is curious to find among the protecting yakkhas such names as Inda, Soma, Varuṇa and Pajāpati, all of whom are great Vedic gods and Bharadvāja who is known as a great Ṛṣi in the Vedic literature.

Protecting Yakkhas-names similar to those of Vedic gods.

We have seen that according to the Dīgha Nikāya all the above gods including the great Brahmā himself were inferior to the Buddha. In fact, throughout the Buddhist literature, we find that the gods including Brahmā came on their visits to the Buddha in order to do him homage or sometimes to carry out some of his orders. We learn from the Khuddakapāṭha Commentary that the gods came on such visits after mid-night. (Khuddakapāṭha Commentary, p. 114).

The Buddha superior to all gods.

The Aṅguttara Nikāya says explicitly that the Cātummahārājika devas, the Tusita, Yāma, Tāvatiṁsa, Nimmānarati and Paranimmita-vasavattī devas who have strong faith in the Buddha, Dhamma and Saṁgha and can

Faith in the Buddha leads to the attainment of sambodhi.

claim to have acquired the stage of sotāpanna, are not liable to fall into hell but are destined for the attainment of sambodhi. (Aṅguttara Nikāya, Vol. III., p. 333). In another part of the Aṅguttara Nikāya we are told that Yama, the ruler of the Yāma heaven, wished to be born down here upon earth in order to get the benefit of receiving the sacred dhamma from the Buddha and thereby improve his own condition. (Aṅguttara Nikāya, Vol. I., p. 142). The Aṅguttara Nikāya (I. 142) tells us that King Yama after seeing various punishments of the sinners, thought thus, " people commit sins in the world and they are punished in consequence thereof." He expressed his desire to become a human being and serve the Tathāgata who might appear on earth and hear him preaching the dhamma and realise it.

Yama's desire to serve the Tathāgata.

In another section of the Aṅguttara Nikāya the Exalted One says repeatedly that Sakka, the ruler of the devas, was the person whose rāga, dosa and moha (passion, hatred and delusion) had not yet left him and therefore he was much inferior to a Bhikkhu who had reached Arahatship and was free from the defects of ordinary beings. (Vol. I., pp. 144-145).

Sakka inferior to an Arahat.

In the Mahāparinibbāṇa Suttanta (Dīgha Nikāya, II., p. 96) the Licchavi nobles who were accoutred in dresses of various dazzling

The Licchavis compared with Tāvatiṁsa gods.

colours, such as, red, white, blue, etc., are compared to the Tāvatiṁsa gods, they are put up by the Buddha as living illustrations of the happy and enviable life in the paradises as popularly known. A similar comparison of the Licchavis with the Tāvatiṁsa gods is also made in the Mahāvastu-avadāna. (Vol. I., p. 262 and vide my work "Some Kṣatriya Tribes of Ancient India, pp. 54-55).

Powers and short-comings of gods.

Gods possessing great and miraculous power and great influence can shake the earth. (Dīgha Nikāya, Vol. II., p. 108). The same Suttanta tells us that the gods living in the sky, who are conscious of the earth, and the gods living on the earth, who are conscious of the earth, are subject to grief and lamentation like ordinary human beings while the gods who are free from attachment are not subject to grief although they are conscious of it and have knowledge of the impermanence of things. (Dīgha Nikāya, Vol. II., pp. 139-140).

We have seen that Sakka was the ruler of the Tāvatimsa gods according to the Dīgha Nikāya (Dīgha Nikāya, Vol. II., p. 263). The Dhammapada Commentary explains the various names of Sakka with their significance. Buddhaghosa here explains

The meaning of the various names of Sakka as explained in the Dhammapada commentary.

that Sakka is called *Maghavā*, a shortened form of *Maghamānava* because he was a human being in the past; he is called

Purindada, because he makes gifts or dāna first. He is named Sakka inasmuch as he practises charity with strong faith, and *Vāsava* because he offered an *āvāsa* or dwelling place. He won the name of *Sahassakkho* for himself, because of his power to think of a thousand things at the same time and he is called *Sujampati* from the name of his wife Sujātā, a daughter of the king of the Asuras. According to the Brahmanic mythology, the name of his wife is Śacī and Sujā is evidently a different reading of the name Śacī which is found in the Ṛgveda itself. And Śacī is the daughter of the Asura Puloma according to the Brahmanical myths, so that there is no difference here. The concrete conception of a thousand eyes in the Hindu myth has been changed into an abstract conception of the power to attend to a thousand things at one and the same time. According to Buddhaghosa, Sakka is so called because he acquired the state of a Sakka after fulfilling seven vows (Dhammapada Commentary, Vol. I., pt. II., pp. 264-265).

The Majjhima Nikāya thus describes the Vejayanta palace of Inda :—

Vejayanta described.

Inda said to Moggallāna thus, "I have built the Vejayanta palace after defeating the asuras in a battle between the devas and the asuras. It consists of one hundred crests each having seven hundred Kūṭāgāras (pinnacled rooms). Each Kūṭāgāra contains seven times seven dancing girls. Each dancing girl has seven times seven female attendants." (Majjhiṁa Nikāya, Vol. I., p. 253).

The course of discipline for acquiring the state of Sakka.

The Saṁyutta Nikāya prescribes that for acquiring the state of Sakka, it was necessary to observe seven *vatas* or vows for going through courses of discipline :—

1. service to parents throughout one's own life
2. respect for the elders of the family
3. speaking sweet words
4. not speaking malicious words
5. remaining free from stinginess
6. speaking the truth throughout life
7. not cherishing anger throughout life
8. checking anger when it arises.

(Saṁyutta Nikāya, Vol. I., p. 228).

The parisās or assemblies of the gods.

In the Mahāparinibbāṇa Suttanta the Buddha mentions that the gods had their parisā or assemblies which are as follows :

1. Cātummahārājika parisā, the assembly of the Cātummahārājika gods
2. Tāvatiṁsaparisā, the assembly of the Tāvatiṁsa gods
3. Māraparisā, the assembly of Māra
4. Brahmaparisā, the assembly of Brahmā

(Dīgha Nikāya, Vol. II., p. 109).

It was in such an assembly of the Tāvatiṁsa gods, that the question of the birth of the Bodhisatta was discussed and arrangements made for his descent on earth according to the Lalita Vistara. The *pariṣad* or the assembly was an important political institution with the Ksatriya tribes that lived in eastern India at the time that Buddhism originated. The pariṣad was also a very important institution with the Vedic Aryans.

Duties of ministers and members of the assembly of the Cātummahārājika devas.

The Aṅguttara Nikāya tells us that the ministers and members of the assembly of the Cātummahārājika devas, wander about on earth on the eighth day of the moon every fortnight, enquiring whether among men there were persons who performed good deeds by showing respect to their parents and the Samaṇas and Brāhmaṇas and whether they observed the fast as required by the Buddhist canon. It is added that on the fourteenth day of the moon, the sons (puttā) of the four Mahārājās also went about wandering over the earth on the same mission. On the fifteenth day of the moon, it is said that the four Mahārājās themselves go about enquiring whether men were observing the uposatha. It is said that the four Mahārājās then present themselves at the sabhā called Sudhamma of the Tāvatiṁsa gods and submit a report about the small or large number of men whom they find observing the uposatha properly and performing the good deeds as mentioned above. (Aṅguttara Nikāya, Vol. I., pp. 142-143).

Many stories are told in Buddhist literature of men who often after death and sometimes even while living on earth, paid visits to the heavens.

King Nimi's visit to heaven.

The Nimi Jātaka relates that King Nimi went to heaven and saw the following sights:—

1. Bīraṇīvimāna, a garden full of trees, flowers, kapparukkha, ponds, etc.
2. Soṇadinna devaputta's seven gold vimānas
3. Phalikavimāna
4. Maṇivimāna
5. Veḷuriyavimāna

He went to the Sumeru mountain and visited seven mountains surrounding it, which were the habitations of the Cātummahārājikadevas. Thence he went to the Tāvatiṁsa devaloka where he saw the image of Inda. Thence he went to the Mote-Hall of the gods, which was well built, artistically beautiful, divided into eight parts having pillars of *lapis lazuli*. Inda and other gods came to receive Nimi and he was given his seat by the side of Inda, the chief of the gods (Nimi Jātaka, Fausboll, Vol. VI., p. 104 foll).

The Acchariyabbhutadhamma Suttaṁ of the Majjhima Nikāya narrates how the Bodhisatta came down from the Tusita Heaven to be born here upon the earth. When the Bodhisatta entered the womb of Queen Māyā leaving the Tusita heaven, a very bright light appeared illuminating the deva, Brahmā and the human worlds, etc. It was more brilliant than the heavenly light. By the help of the light the beings of one world could see the beings of another world. After the birth of the Bodhisatta, four gods came from four quarters to guard the Bodhisatta and his mother against human or non-human foes. (Majjhima Nikāya, Vol. III., p. 120). Similarly in the Lalita Vistara we read that when the Bodhisatta fallen from the Tusita heaven, entered the womb of Māyā, a lotus extending up to the Brahmaloka appeared, which became visible to Mahābrahmā alone. (Lalitávistara, Ed. by Lefmann, p. 64). Again we read that when the Bodhisatta entered Māyā's womb, the earth with its forest trembled six times, golden lustre spread all round, all sins were removed, the gods became delighted, a well-decorated chariot appeared and the charioteer stood motionless in it (Ibid., p. 72). For seven nights holy lustre extended up to the Brahmaloka (Ibid, p. 74).

Gods and Bodhisatta's birth.

The Aṅguttara Nikāya furnishes a good deal of information about the meritorious deeds qualifying men to be translated to the various regions of heaven. The Enlightened One tells Sāriputta on one occasion : " He who practises charity without freeing himself from the

Merits entitling people to reach various regions of heaven.

taint of selfishness, being attached to the object of charity, hoping for wealth and enjoyment in after-life, in consequence of such charity, after death will be reborn in the heaven of the Cātummahārājika gods. Those among the Cātummahārājikas, the Tusitas, Yāmas, Tāvatiṁsas, the Nimmānaratis and the Paranimmitavasavattins who have acquired strong faith in the Buddha, the Dhamma and the Saṁgha, may be said to have acquired the state of *Sotāpanna*, they are not liable to fall into hell and are destined to attain sambodhi (Aṅguttara Nikāya, Vol. III., pp. 332-333).

Similarly in the same Nikāya we are told of a great Buddhist teacher of the name of Sunetta who had many lay disciples. Preaching to his pupils about the means of winning the Brahmaloka, he taught that those among his disciples who could thoroughly comprehend and grasp his teachings, would be entitled to reach the heaven of Brahmā, but those who failed to appreciate them fully would enter the regions of the six lower heavens. (Aṅguttara Nikāya, Vol. IV., pp. 103-104).

Buddhaghosa's view.

Buddhaghosa in his Visuddhimagga states the circumstances under which men may attain to heaven. A person performs meritorious deeds for the attainment of heavenly bliss and in consequence of such deeds, he is reborn in heaven (Vol. I., p. 199). A person who is an observer of the precepts formulated by the great teacher and is devoted to the practice of these precepts, is reborn in heaven after death and dissolution of the body. (Vol. I., p. 9). It is stated in that work that sīla or precept is the best ladder by which one may reach the regions of the gods. (Vol. I., p. 10). In another place Buddhaghosa observes that a person is reborn in heaven by meditating on Buddha's qualities. (Vol. I., p. 213). The Visuddhimagga observes that even the lower animals can attain to heaven; it records that a frog that attentively listened to the teachings of the Buddha, was born after death in a golden mansion in the Tāvatiṁsa heaven and was named Maṇḍukadevaputta having 1,000 apsarasas as his wives. This devaputta appeared before the Buddha in his vimāna, and he made it the occasion for a religious discourse, after listening to which the devaputta reached the first stage of sanctification. (Vol. I., pp. 208-209).

Rewards and punishments.

The Pañcagatidīpanaṁ also furnishes some information regarding heaven. It states that among the gods, men and demons, those who are malicious do not live long, but those who are free from malice, attain long life. Those who oppress others by confining and beating them, are subject to leprosy, madness, etc. Those who misappropriate the property of others and do not make gifts to anybody, cannot earn money even with great effort. Those who give stolen wealth to others at first become rich but are afterwards reduced to poverty. Those who acquire wealth by honest means but do not give it to anybody, get wealth with great effort. Those who do not steal wealth but are very charitable, obtain wealth which cannot be destroyed by theft, etc. Those who offer food daily are long-lived, endowed with beauty, strength, intelligence, health and happiness. Those who offer clothes become shy, beautiful, pure, and obtain clothes. Those who offer houses or shelters obtain palaces full of wealth. Those who offer carriages, palanquins, shoes, etc., always become happy and get the most comfortable conveyances. Those who dig wells, tanks, etc., and thus provide water to the public, always become free from suffering and are not troubled with thirst. Those who offer gardens are worshipped with various kinds of flowers and become wealthy and beautiful. Those who make a gift of their learning by imparting it to others can easily acquire learning. Those who offer medicine always become free from disease. Those who offer lights acquire knowledge. Those who offer beds and seats always enjoy happiness. Those who offer milch cows become long-lived and are endowed with strength, beauty, etc. Those who make gifts of daughters to suitable bridegrooms obtain whatever they desire. Those who offer land obtain wealth, crops etc. Those who do not commit adultery but whose mind is inclined towards the wives of others will be reborn as females. Those women who hate women, who are pious and not licentious and always pray for manhood, are reborn as men. Those who always abuse others and are liars, are reborn as hunch-backs and dwarfs. Those who are dull in intelligence and full of malice are reborn as deaf men. Those who do not distinguish between good and bad are reborn as fools (J.P.T.S., 1884, pp. 158-160). Those who do not seek their own personal happiness, who are not elated by depriving others of their happiness, become the best of grahas (planets) and mahārājās. Those who revere their parents, who are charitable and who are ready to pardon others, who do not find delight in quarrels are reborn in the Tāvatiṁsa heaven. Those who are not fond of fights and dissensions, etc., and always do good deeds, go to Yāmaloka. Those who are endowed with much knowledge of the sacred lore (bahussutas), and are dhammadharas, wise, aspire to salvation, and always find delight in good things, go to Tusita heaven. Those who offer precepts to others and themselves observe them, are ardent to do good deeds, go to the Nimmānarati heaven. Those who are energetic and active, controlled and restrained, go to the Paranimmitavasavattī heaven. By observing precepts a person goes to heaven, by meditation

Merits that lead to the different grades of heaven.

one goes to Brahmaloka and by true knowledge one obtains Nirvāṇa (Ibid., p. 160).

Instances of persons attaining various grades of the heavens according to their deeds.

We read in the Aṅguttara Nikāya that a Bhikkhu named Tissa was reborn after death in the Brahmaloka and was known there as Tissa Brahmā and it is said that he was endowed with miraculous power, and possessed great influence (Aṅguttara Nikāya, Vol. III., p.332). Buddhaghosa points out in the Sumaṅgalavilāsinī that King Bimbisāra of Magadha was after death reborn in the Cātummahārājika heaven as a companion of Vessavana under the name of Janavasabha. (Vol. I., p. 137). The Manorathapuraṇī, a commentary on the Aṅguttara Nikāya by Buddhaghosa, also relates a story about a person who visited heaven. A person named Damiḷa went to heaven after worshipping ākāsacaitya (*i.e.* the caitya erected by Inda in the sky on the hair of the Bodhisatta cut off on the bank of the river Anomā). A certain person obtained heaven as the reward of his offering a piece of cloth to a young Bhikkhu. Those persons in heaven who cannot remember the meritorious deeds done by them while on earth, are reminded of them by the devadūtas. In case the devadūtas fail to do this, Yama makes them remember the meritorious deeds done by them while on earth. Once a minister worshipped a mahācaitya and offered the merit of this act to Yama but he had to go to hell because of some misdeeds done by him. He was brought before Yama by the devadūtas. Yama asked him whether he had accumulated any merit on earth but he could not recollect anything. Yama asked him whether he could remember having worshipped the mahācaitya; this he remembered and went to heaven. Had Yama not made him recall his deeds of merit and if he could not find anything of merit done by that person, Yama would have been very sorry, as the man would have suffered much in hell. (Manorathapuraṇī, Sinhalese edition, p. 207).

Further instances from Buddhaghosa's Dhammapada commentary.

The Dhammapada Commentary which, in our view, was compiled by Buddhaghosa, relates some stories about the heavens like those narrated in the Petavatthu Commentary. There is a reference to Mahākassapa absorbed in nirodhasamāpatti. On the seventh day he got up from the samāpatti and went out for alms. A woman guarding a paddy field, offered to Mahākassapa the fried rice which she was taking for her husband. Owing to this meritorious deed, she was reborn in the Tāvatiṁsa heaven in a golden mansion extending over 30 yojanas (Vol. III., pp. 6-7).

A devatā living on the gate of Anāthapiṇḍika's house, warned the seṭṭhi that he should not make such profuse gifts to the Buddhist Saṁgha, as he would thereby run the risk of becoming poorer day by day. The seṭṭhi did not listen to his words and the devatā was deprived of his abode because of his envy towards the Buddha. The devatā in vain sought refuge in the heaven of the four mahārājās and then of Sakka who asked him to return to the seṭṭhi and get his pardon by securing for him the lost treasure (Vol. III., pp. 10, 11, 12, and 13). A banker named Kukkuṭamitta offered himself with his family and all the wealth he had, to the service of a dagoba containing Kassapa Buddha's relics. As a result Kukkuṭamitta and the sixteen members of his family were reborn in heaven (Vol. III., pp. 24-30). Once a son of the king of Benares took a vow that he would worship a tree-god dwelling on a nigrodha tree by sacrificing before him 100 rājās of Jambudīpa with their chief queens. On his succession to the throne of his father, he went to worship the tree-god with all the rājās and their chief queens except Dinnā, chief queen of Uggasena, as she was in an advanced stage of pregnancy at that time. The tree-god seemed disinclined to accept the offering of the king as Dinnā was not brought. The king brought Dinnā before the god but he refrained from killing so many human beings, after being instructed by her with regard to the baneful effect of such deeds on one's claim to go to heaven. (Vol. II., pp. 14-17). In the past a sāmaṇera named Suka was born as a devaputta for offering food to a paccekabuddha (Vol. III., pp. 94-95). Mallikā, queen of King Pasenadi of Kosala, committed adultery only once but she concealed the offence by telling lies to the King. She repented and died. After death she suffered in the Avīci hell for seven days but on account of the great merit which she had accumulated by her good deeds during her life time, she was reborn as a goddess in the Tusita heaven. (D.C., Vol. III., pp. 119-21). From the Anāthapiṇḍikaputtakālavatthu we learn that the fruition of the first stage of sanctification is superior to heaven. (D.C., Vol. III., p. 191). Nandiya was a faithful upāsaka of the Buddha. He used to make good offerings to the bhikkhusaṁgha, to the poor and the destitute. A well-furnished ārāma was offered by him to the Buddha and his disciples. In consequence of this he was reborn after death in a golden palace full of seven kinds of gems in the Tāvatiṁsa heaven. (D.C., Vol. III., pp. 290-291). Rohiṇī, sister of Anuruddha, had to suffer for some time from a skin disease on account of her sin but on the advice of Anuruddha, she built a hall for the bhikkhus and used to sweep its floor every day. In consequence of this merit, she was cured of her disease and after death was reborn in the Tāvatiṁsa heaven. Afterwards she became a wife of Sakka. (D.C., Vol. III., pp. 295-297). Ubbarī, a king's daughter, was reborn in the Brahmaloka on account of her attainment of the first stage of meditation but owing to some evil deeds done in her former existence, she fell down from the Brahmaloka and in time she was reborn as a pig but she was again reborn as a paribbājikā at Rājagaha; but again she fell down from that stage and was reborn in the family of a banker as a result of the attainment of the first stage of meditation. In the thirteenth birth she attained arahatship after having obtained ordination in the teachings of the Buddha. (D.C., Vol. IV., pp. 46-47). A banker of Sāvatthī named Tagara in his former existence offered food to a paccekabuddha. In consequence of this meritorious deed he was reborn seven times in heaven. (D.C., Vol. IV., pp. 77 foll).

The Abhidhammattha-Saṅgaha, a later compendium, describes the popular cosmography of the Buddhists in the following manner:

The popular Cosmography as described in the Abhidhammattha-Saṅgaha.

There are four Apāyabhumis and seven Kāmasugatibhumis which constitute the Kāmaloka or Kāmāvacaraloka. The four apāyas are :—

1. Niraya 2. Tiracchānayoni 3. Pettivisaya 4. Asurakāya. The seven Kāmasugatibhumis are :—

1. Manussā 2. Cātummahārājikā 3. Tāvatiṁsā 4. Yāmā 5. Tusitā 6. Nimmānarati 7. Paranimmitavasavattī. Higher than the Kāmaloka there is the Rūpaloka which is divided into sixteen lokas. Higher than the Rūpaloka there is the Arūpaloka (Abhidhammattha Saṅgaha, Kosambī's Ed., Chap. 5.).

With regard to these worlds, the persons who are qualified to be reborn there as well as the period during which the gods can live in any particular world, we have an interesting statement in the Vibhaṅga. Here at first the gods are divided into three groups thus :—

" There are three kinds of gods :—

1. Sammatidevā are devas who are admitted as such by all *e.g.* kings, queens, princes.

2. Uppattidevā are all gods commencing from the Cātummahārājika-devas up to the Akaniṭṭha-brahmadevas.

3. Visuddhidevas are all arahats.

The space of life allowed to various grades of gods.

The lease of life of the Cātummahārājikadevas is 90,00,000 years. It is to be noted that 50 years in the human world are equal to one day and night in the Cātummahārājika heaven. The lease of life of the Tāvatiṁsa gods is 3 koṭis and 60,00,000 years; 100 years in the human world are equal to one day and night among these gods. The lease of life of the Yama gods is 14 koṭis and 40,00,000 years, 200 years in the human world are equal to one day and night among them. The lease of life of the Tusita gods is 57 koṭis and 60,00,000 years and 400 years in the human world are equal to one day and night among them. The lease of life of the Nimmānaratidevas is 203 koṭis and 40,00,000 years, 800 years in the human world are equal to one day and night among them; the lease of life of the Paranimmitavasavattī devas is 921 koṭis and 60,00,000 years, 1,600 years in the human world are equal to one day and night among these gods.

Lease of life according to different stages of meditation.

Those who slightly meditate in the first stage of meditation (paṭhamajhāna) will be born among the Brahmapārisajja gods. The lease of life of these gods is one third part of a kappa. Those who reach the midway of the first stage of meditation will be born among the Brahmapurohita gods. Their lease of life is one half of a kappa. Those who meditate fully in the first stage of meditation will be born among Mahābrahmā gods and their lease of life is one kappa.

Those who slightly meditate in the second stage of meditation will be born among the Parittābha gods and their lease of life is two kappas. Those who reach midway in the second stage of meditation will be born among the Appamānābha gods and their lease of life is four kappas; those who fully meditate in the second stage of meditation will be born among Ābhassara gods and their lease of life is eight kappas. Those who slightly meditate in the third stage of meditation will be born among the Parittasubha gods and their lease of life is sixteen kappas; those who reach the midway in the third stage will be born among the Appamānasubha gods and their lease of life thirty-two kappas or kalpas; those who fully meditate in the third stage of meditation will be born among the Subhakinna gods and their lease of life, sixty-four kalpas. Some of those who meditate in the fourth stage of meditation will be Asaññasattadevas, some will be born as Vehapphala gods; some Avīha gods, some Atappa gods, some Sudassa gods, some Sudassī gods, some Akaniṭṭha gods, some Ākāsañcāyatanūpaga gods, some Viññāṇañcāyatanūpaga gods, some Ākiñcaññāyatanūpaga gods and some Nevasaññānasaññāyatanūpaga gods according to their different objects of meditation, different modes of thought, different inclinations, different applications, different understanding and wisdom. The lease of life of Asaññasatta and Vehapphala gods is 500 kappas each. The lease of life of Avīha gods is 1,000 kalpas, the lease of life of Atappa gods is 2,000 kalpas, the lease of life of Sudassa gods is 4,000 kalpas, the lease of life of Sudassī gods is 8,000 kalpas, the lease of life of Akaniṭṭha gods is 16,000 kalpas, the lease of life of Ākāsanañcāyatanūpa gods is 20,000 kalpas, the lease of life of Viññāṇañcāyatanūpaga gods is 40,000 kalpas, the lease of life of Ākiñcaññāyatanūpaga gods is 60,000 kalpas and the lease of life of the Nevasaññānasaññāyatanūpaga gods is 84,000 kalpas. (Vibhaṅga, P. T. S. edition, pp. 422-426, cf. also Anguttara Nikāya, Vol. I., pp. 213-214; Ibid., Vol. I., pp. 267-68).

The length of life of the gods is also enumerated in the Abhidhammattha-Saṅgaha. The lease of life of the Cātummahārājika gods is 90,00,000, that of the Tāvatiṁsa gods is four times longer than the Cātummahārājika gods, next higher gods live four times longer than the Tāvatiṁsa gods and so on up to the Paranimmitavasavattī gods. The lease of life of the Brahmapārisajja gods is one-third of a kappa, that of the Brahmapurohita gods is half of a kappa, that of Mahābrahma is one kappa, that of the Parittābhadevas is two kappas, next higher gods live four kalpas and so on up to the Subhakinna gods. Vehapphala and Asaññasatta gods live 500 kalpas and the Avīha gods live 1,000 kalpas. Atappā gods live 2000 kalpas, Sudassā gods, 4,000 kalpas, Sudassī gods 8,000 kalpas and the Akaniṭṭha gods, 16,000 kalpas, Ākāsānañcāyatanūpaga gods, 20,000 kalpas, Viññānañcāyatanūpaga gods, 40,000 kalpas, Ākiñcaññāyatanūpaga gods, 60,000 kalpas and the Nevasaññānasaññāyatanūpaga gods, 84,000 kalpas. (Abhidhammattha-Saṅgaha, Kosambī's Ed. Chap. 5).

In the earlier literature of the Pāli-Buddhist Tripiṭaka also we have the similar enumeration of the length of life of the six-classes of the Kāmāvacara devas beginning from the Cātummahārājika devas to the Paranimmitavasavattī devas in the Aṅguttara Nikāya, in a discourse delivered by the Buddha to Visākhā, the rich lady of Śrāvastī.

Prof. Poussin's note on the ideas of the Sarvāstivādin School ie: the situation and extent of the heavens and the life-period of the gods.

The ideas of the Sarvāstivādin school about the situation and extent of the heavens and the life-period of the gods have been compiled by Prof. Louis de la Vallee Poussin from the *Abhidharmakoṣavyākhyā*, a commentary on the Abhidharmakoṣa of Vasuvandhu. We are greatly thankful to Dr. Poussin for his valuable note which is given below.

" Heavens of the concupiscence-world (kāmadhātu)—

(a) On the fourth terrace of Meru is the retinue of the Four Great Kings (cāturmahārājakāyikas, catummahārājikas), 80,000 in all (?) and (higher up, if we are to believe Dīgha, 1. 216) the Four Great Kings, rulers of the cardinal points. These are the first beings who regularly receive the name of 'gods,' and are classed as such. The length of their life is five hundred years, a day being equal to fifty human years, and their height is one-fourth krośa ($\frac{1}{8}$ yojana, 'league'). Perhaps the numerous servants and courtiers of the Great Kings, the Gandharvas, 'celestial musicians,' etc., although they are not devas, ought to be regarded as belonging to this category.

Half-way up Meru are the chariots of the sun (51 leagues), of the moon (a league further down), and of the stars. These deities do not form a special class.

(b) On the summit of Meru are the gods 'who have the thirty-three at their head' (trāyastrimśas; tāvatimsas), to the number of 100,000 (?), and, above them (according to Dīgha), is their King Śakra, devānam Inda, 'the Indra of the gods.' Their town, 'Lovely view,' is 2,500 miles square, and contains the Palace of Victory (Vaijayanta) [Majjhima, 1. 253, etc.]. They live for 1,000 years, one day being equal to 100 human years (Dīgha, II, 327), and their height is ½ krośa.

Then there are palaces which might be called aerial (vimāna).

(c) 160,000 leagues above Jambudvīpa, i.e. 80,000 above the thirty-three, and 80,000 leagues broad, the palace of the Yāma gods, whose king Suyāma, according to Dīgha, dwells higher up. Length of life, 2,000 years, one day=200 human years; height, ¾ krośa.

(d) The abode of the Tuṣitas, 'satisfied' or 'blissful'; the residence of a future Buddha before his last existence; king, Samtusita; length of life, 4,000 years; height, one krośa.

(e) The abode of the Nirmānaratis, 'who have their pleasure in creation,' 'happy creators'; king, Sunirmita, 'well-built.' According to the A. K. V., the meaning of this name is 'enjoying self-created pleasures,' in contrast with the inferior gods, who enjoy objects which are presented to them on account of the deserts (of. Itivuttaka, p. 94). Length of life, 8,000 years; height, 1¼ krośa.

(f) 1,280,000 leagues above Jambudvīpa, 640,000 leagues broad, the abode of the 60,000 Paranirmitavaśavartins (paranirmita, and sometimes wrongly (?) pari), having Vaśavartin, 'the sovereign' as king (Dīgha, 1. 219). The name of these gods means 'rulers over the things created by others,' 'disposers of others' creations' (C.A.F. Rhys Davids' tr.), i.e. they themselves create or they cause others to create, the objects of enjoyment which they desire. Length of life, 160,000 years, one day=16,000 human years; height, 1½ krośa.

(i) " First-Trance heavens—(1) Brahmapārṣadyas (or kāyikas), retinue of Brahmā; length of life, 20 small ages of the world (20 antarakalpas =¼ great kalpa): height, ½ league. The heaven is situated 2,580,000 leagues above Jambudvīpa, and is 1,290,000 leagues broad. These numbers have to be doubled for the following heavens.

(ii) " Second-Trance Heavens—(1) Parīttābhas (' Limited splendour'); length of life, 2 kalpas; height, 2 leagues. These figures are doubled for the next five classes. (2) Apramāṇābhas, 'Immeasurable splendour.' (3) Ābhāśvaras (Ābhassara), 'Radiant.'

(iii) Third-Trance Heavens (1) Parittaśubhas, 'limited beauty.' (2) Apramāṇaśubhas, 'immeasurable beauty.' (3) Subhakṛtsṇas (Subhakiṇha, wrongly Subhakiṇṇa), 'Complete beauty'; length of life, 64 kalpas, i.e. until the return of the destruction of the cosmos by wind (see Ages of the World—(Buddhist), Vol. I., p. 188); height, 64 leagues.

(iv) "Fourth-Trance Heavens—(1) Anabhrakas ('Cloudless'); 125 kalpas and leagues (not 128, which would be double that of the Subhakṛtsṇas); these numbers are doubled for the following classes.

(2) Puṇyaprasavas, 'Merit-born' (Tib.bsod-nams-skyes), or perhaps 'Merit-begetting' (?). (3) Bṛhatphalas (Vehapphalas), 'Abundant fruit.' (4)-(8) bear the generic name of Śuddhāvāsa, 'Pure abode' whence Śuddhāvāsikas, Śuddhāvāsa-kāyikas, 'inhabitants of the Pure abodes'. (4) Avṛhas (Avihas), 'Effortless,' (?) (5) Atapas (atappa = atāpya), 'No heat,' 'Cool gods.' (6) Sudṛśas (Sudassa), 'Beautiful.' (7) Sudarśana (Sudassin), 'well-seeing.' (8) Akaniṣṭhas, 'Sublime' (= 'not youngest,' 'not smallest'), also called (or subordinated to) Aghanisthas, at the end (nistha), of the compact (agha), i.e. 'at the top or the end of the material world'; length of life, 16,000 kalpas; height, 16,000 leagues.

The total number of 'stages' in the rūpa world.

"The total number of 'places' or 'stages' in the rūpa world, therefore, is seventeen, according to the Abhidharmakoṣa, iii. 2; the Kashmīrians suppress one of them. The Pāli tradition of Abhidharma counts only sixteen; it has neither the Anabhrakas nor the Puṇyaprasavas, but it adds the Asaṁjñasattvas (devas, 'unconscious beings,' 'gods') as follows:

Fourth Trance—(1) Asaññasattas, (2) Vehapphalas, (3) Pure abodes, five in number. (In later documents, e. g. in the Abhidhammatthasamgaha V. 2-6, 10, tr. Warren, Buddhism, p. 289, the Asaññasattas come after the Vehapphalas; and the same arrangement occurs in Northern texts, viz. Lalitavistara, p. 150, Dharmasaṅgraha, 128, Beal p. 85 (according to Dīrghāgama ?), which add the Asaṁjñasattvas to the list of the Kośa).

Lastly, certain sources place the heaven of Mahāmaheśvara, the Great Lord, Śīva, above the Akaniṣṭhas—a non-Buddhist idea borrowed from Hinduism." (Hastings, Encyclopædia of Religion and Ethics, Vol. IV., pp. 134-136).

SECTION II

Illustrative stories from the Vimānavatthu Commentary

When the Buddha was residing at Sāvatthī in the ārāma of Anāthapiṇḍika at Jetavana, King Pasenadi of Kosala, for one week, made gifts on an immense scale, not to be compared with the charity practised by anybody in his kingdom and so it was known as asadisadāna (incomparable charity). To imitate this, Anāthapiṇḍika and Visākhā each made liberal gifts for three days. Their charities became known all over the Jambudīpa and following them, the people of Jambudīpa began to offer food, drink, seats, etc., to samaṇas, brāhmaṇas, the poor and the destitute. At that time a bhikkhu who was on his round for alms, reached a certain house at the time of breakfast. A daughter of that house was a great believer in the Buddha. She, out of great devotion, welcomed the bhikkhu and offered him a seat (a pīṭha, wooden tool) covered with a very nice cloth and when he was seated there at ease, offered him food and eventually the girl made a gift of that seat to the thera. In consequence of this meritorious deed, she after death was reborn in a golden vimāna or mansion which extended over 12 yojanas in the

Pīṭhavimāna.

Tāvatiṁsa heaven and a thousand apsarases were appointed to attend on her. Besides, in consequence of her making a gift of a pīṭha to the bhikkhu, she was awarded, in the Tāvatiṁsa heaven, a golden couch which could carry her through the heavens at a great speed. (Vimānavatthu commentary, pp. 5-6).

A woman of Sāvatthī seeing a thera come to her house for alms, most gladly offered him a seat covered with a piece of blue cloth with the result that she obtained in heaven a vimāna made up of veḷuriya (*lapis lazuli*) which was a kind of gem of a dazzling blue colour like that of the neck of the peacock. In that vimāna she sped through the heavens, bright and shining like lightning. (Ibid, 26-27).

An arahant of Rājagaha, after having obtained alms, came to a house, the door of which was open, with the intention of sitting and eating his food there. A woman who was the mistress of the house, gladly welcomed him and gave him a pīṭha to sit on, covered with yellow cloth, praying that by this meritorious deed she might obtain a gold pīṭha. She told the thera while he was about to leave the house after he had finished his repast that she had presented the seat to him and he should take it away with him. The thera took it and offered it to the Saṁgha. The mistress of the house, after death, was reborn in the golden mansion of the Tāvatiṁsa heaven and obtained a golden couch there. (Vimānavatthu commentary, pp. 27-28).

Kuñjaravimāna.

When the Buddha was at Kālandakanivāpa at Veluvana near Rājagaha, it was announced that a festival would be held there. The people of the city began to sweep the streets, decorate houses, each according to the length of his purse. The city appeared to be beautiful like a city of the gods. King Bimbisāra came out of his palace with a large retinue and a display of royal splendour and marched with great pomp round the city. A daughter of a family of Rājagaha, moved at the spectacle, enquired in her own mind what merit had qualified the king for the acquisition of so much wealth and power. She asked the learned about it and was told that "the effect of dāna or gift is like the kapparukkha (i.e. the tree which fulfils every wish) or the cintāmaṇi that converts the baser metals into gold." Hearing this, her mind was filled with an eager desire to offer charity. At that time her parents sent her a pair of new cloth, a new tool and a pair of lotus, clarified butter, honey, rice, sugar, etc. She on receipt of these articles was with a joyous heart preparing to offer charity. She prepared rice-gruel with honey and various kinds of food and drink and decorated the place where the bhikkhus would be given charity. She prepared seats there, covered with white cloth, decorating the legs of the seats with blooming lotuses. After bathing herself, and putting on beautiful cloth, she sent her maid-servants to invite a bhikkhu who was going round for alms. The maid-servant saw Sāriputta and invited him to her house. The daughter with great devotion welcomed the thera, made him sit on the decorated seat and offered him the food already prepared by her. While offering charity, she prayed that by virtue of the merit acquired by her for this gift she might be blessed with celestial gifts including an elephant, a kūṭāgāra (pinnacled house), bed, etc. When the thera was going away after taking food, she presented him new clothes and sent men carrying a couch to the vihāra where he dwelt. In consequence of this merit, she after death, was reborn in the golden mansion of the Tāvatiṁsa heaven with a retinue of a thousand heavenly maidens (apsaras) and she saw there lotuses all around her. She also received a well-decorated elephant and golden couch. She used to go for a walk in the Nandanavana, seated on this celestial elephant. One day on her way to the vana, she met Moggallāna and being asked, related to him how she had acquired such celestial splendour. (Vimānavatthu commentary, p. 31 foll).

Nāvāvimāna.

When the Buddha was at Sāvatthī, some sixteen bhikkhus spent the rainy season in a village hermitage.

They, in summer, set out for Sāvatthī filled with a desire to be blessed with a sight of the Master and to listen to the Dhamma from his own mouth. On the way they had to pass through a waterless desert. Tired with the heat and parched with thirst as they were trudging past a village, they saw a woman going with a water-pot to fetch water from a well. They followed the woman with the hope of finding water. They sat in a place a little away from the spot where the woman was drawing water. When the woman had filled the pitchers, the bhikkhus attracted her attention and thinking that they must be suffering from thirst, out of great devotion she offered water to them which they took from her in a pot; they slaked their thirst and cooled themselves by washing their hands and expressed their appreciation of the offering of water by the woman. She, after death, was reborn in the Tāvatiṁsa heaven by virtue of that merit and there got a vimāna with a kapparukkha. A beautiful streamlet with cold water was flowing through the garden. On both sides of the streamlet there were big ponds full of lotuses of five colours and there were golden boats. The Goddess used to sport in the boat and was met by Mahāmoggallāna whom she told how she was born in that vimāna. (Vimānavatthu commentary, pp. 40-41).

When the Lord was residing at Sāvatthī, a thera free from sins, came out of the city with the intention of passing the *vassa* at a village hermitage. But tired and thirsty, he could not reach that village but came to another hamlet on the way. Finding no shady place or water outside the village, he entered it and stood before the gate of a house. A woman of the house, noticing him invited him to enter the house and finding him tired and thirsty offered him a seat and brought him water to wash his feet with and also oil to rub them with. Shortly afterwards she brought a well-scented cold drink for him. The thera after cooling himself with the drink, left her after approving her offering. She, after death, was reborn in the Tāvatiṁsa heaven and was blessed with the same joys as the lady mentioned in the preceding story. (Vimānavatthu commentary, p. 44).

Once the Buddha, on his tour through the Kosala country, went to a brahmin village named Thūṇa. The Brahmins were not well-disposed towards the Buddha and were very envious. They feared that if the Buddha came and resided in their village for two or three days, he would convert all the villagers to his faith and in that case Brahmanism would disappear from that spot and so they tried various ways to prevent the Buddha's advent. They removed all the boats on the river and destroyed the bridge so that he might not cross over to their place. Moreover, they filled all the wells with earth and grass so that the Buddha and his disciples might not get water to drink. The Buddha felt in his heart pity for them, the erring Brāhmaṇas, and went to the Brahmin village through the sky and sat at the foot of a tree. Many females were going past him to fetch water. The villagers were instructed not to give water or anything else to samaṇa Gotama and his disciples. Among the females going to fetch water, there was a servant girl of a Brahmin; she thought that it was an opportune moment for her to liberate herself from slavery, and careless whether the Brahmins would beat her or even kill her, she offered a pot of water to the Buddha who drank water from it and by his miraculous power the pitcher became full every time its contents were exhausted, so that the disciples quenched their thirst from it. The Buddha in order to increase her faith in him showed that a pot of water given by her was sufficient to quench the thirst of the Buddha and his disciples and he returned the pot full of water to her. The Brahmin master heard all about it and was very angry with her and beat her to death. She, after death, was reborn in the Tāvatiṁsa heaven and was given the other objects of heavenly enjoyment as in the two preceding cases. (Vimānavatthu commentary, pp. 45-47).

On a sabbath day many lay devotees—upāsakas

Dīpavimāna.

and upāsikas—in the forenoon offered various kinds of charity including food and drink and in the afternoon taking various kinds of scents and garlands, went to a vihāra to pay their respects to the worthy bhikkhus. After finishing the worship, they sat down to hear the sermon till dusk. An upāsikā, finding that it was dark, brought a light before the preacher's seat. In consequence of this merit, she with joy in her mind went home and sometime after died and was reborn in the Tāvatiṁsa heaven in Jotirasavimāna. The splendour of the body of this goddess was much brighter than that of others, by virtue of the merit she had acquired by presenting a light. She related her past story to Mahāmoggallāna, when asked. (Vimānavatthu commentary pp. 50-51).

Tiladakkhiṇavimāna.

While the Buddha was at Sāvatthī, a pregnant woman of Rājagaha being desirous of getting pure tila (sesamum) oil, placed tila seeds to dry in the rays of the sun after washing them carefully. Her life-period (āyu) had come to an end that very day and she was destined to fall into hell after death. Early in the morning the Buddha while visualising the earth in his meditation saw this and moved by pity to save her from hell, came to her to accept an offering of tila. The woman seeing the Buddha before her, was filled with delight, saluted him and finding nothing else with which he could make a suitable offering to the Exalted One, collected the sesamum seeds took them in her joined palms and made a present of them to the Buddha who blessed her that she would be happy. She died at dawn and was reborn in a golden vimāna in the Tāvatiṁsa heaven. The goddess related to Mahāmoggallāna her past history when asked. (V. commy. p. 54).

Patibbatāvimāna.

When the Buddha was at Sāvatthī, there was a woman, very faithful and obedient to her husband. She was patient and was not subject to anger. She never used harsh words even when she was irritated, was truthful and had faith in the Buddha. She used to make offerings according to her means. After death, she was reborn in the Tāvatiṁsa heaven. Her palace or vimāna was adorned with things of beauty and joy and she was surrounded by an atmosphere of refinement. There was the Koñca or Krañca, the bird whose constancy in love for the mate is celebrated by poets ; there were the swans of heavenly form and the cuckoo with its sweet coo ; the vimāna was full of flowers on every side, decorated with beautiful objects and full of men and women. She reigned there as a goddess, surrounded by apsarases who danced and sang and made themselves merry in every way. She emitted an effulgence and her beautiful complexion threw a halo of glory all around.

She related her past history to Mahāmoggallāna, when asked, in the following words :—

"I in my human life was always devoted to my husband and used to protect him as a mother protects her son. I never used harsh words although I had occasion to be angry. I was truthful, charitable, and observer of precepts. On account of these I have got such beauty and wealth." (Vimānavatthu commy, pp. 56-57).

A similar story is told of another lady, also hailing from Sāvatthī, who too was loyal at heart to her husband and made gifts as far as she could; she also, after death, was rewarded with a vimāna like the one described above.

Suṇisāvimāna.

At Sāvatthī, an arahat came to a house for alms. The daughter-in-law of the family seeing the arahat, was filled with joy and ardour, and with great devotion offered some portion of the cakes which she had got for her own use. The thera accepted the offering and went away blessing her. In consequence of the merit acquired, she, after death, was reborn in the Tāvatiṁsa heaven. (Vimānavatthu commentary, p. 61).

Uttarāvimāna.

When the Buddha was at Kalandakanivāpa at Veluvana near Rājagaha, a poor man named Puṇṇa was the servant of a banker of Rājagaha. Puṇṇa had only two members in his family, his wife and his daughter both of whom bore the name of

Uttarā. At that time a festival known as the Nakkhattakīam was announced to be held for a week by the people of the town. The banker asked Puṇṇa whether he would take part in the festivities or work in his house. He replied that nakkhattakīam was for the rich and he being a poor man would not be able to participate in the sports. He prayed that if he could get bulls, he would go to the field with them to cultivate it. He was given two strong bulls by his master and with them he went to plough the field. Before going to his hard work he asked his wife to cook double the usual quantity of rice and to take it to the field. At that time as the thera Sāriputta rose up from meditation after a week, looking for some person whom he could bring to the true faith, he saw Puṇṇa to be the fit person to whom he should pay his first visit. Puṇṇa, as soon as he saw Sāriputta, welcomed him cordially, stopped his work and thinking that the gift of a tooth-brush would bring him wealth, gave him a tooth-brush and also some water for ablution. The thera then went towards the town and met Puṇṇa's wife as she was bringing food which she offered to Sāriputta, although the food she was bringing was intended for her husband who would be very hungry at that time on account of his hard work in the field. Sāriputta would accept only half the food offered but the woman desirous of accumulating some merit for the next world, begged him to accept the whole of it. Sāriputta did so and left his blessings with her. Puṇṇa's wife then returned home and again cooked rice for her husband who had become very hungry and was sitting at the foot of a tree eagerly expecting the cooked rice. She came to her husband with food and explaining to him the cause of the delay, prayed to be excused for having kept him waiting so long. Puṇṇa, hearing this, was satisfied and laid himself down to sleep with his head on her lap. After rising from sleep Puṇṇa could hardly believe his eyes when he saw the cultivated field full of gold. He and his wife realised that they had received gold through the influence of the thera Sāriputta. They took some gold to the king and related the whole matter to him. The king sent carts with officers to bring the gold to his treasury but as soon as the gold was put into the cart, it turned into earth. The officers related the matter to the king who realised that the wealth being the reward for the good deeds of the poor family, could be enjoyed by them alone and accordingly ordered his officers to take the gold on behalf of Puṇṇa. The gold was brought into the palace, and piled up there. The king invited the people to look at it and as it made Puṇṇa the richest man in the whole city, he was made the nagaraseṭṭhi with the name Bahudhanaseṭṭhi. Puṇṇa made plentiful gifts to the Buddha and the congregation on the occasion of his being installed as seṭṭhi and his entrance into the new palace. Puṇṇa and his wife attained the first stage of sanctification by their meritorious deeds.

Puṇṇa's daughter Uttarā was married to the son of the banker whom Puṇṇa had served before. Puṇṇa's daughter was not happy in the house of her father-in-law who was a false believer and she had no opportunity of making any gifts to the bhikkhus and the congregation. She informed her father of her difficulty. Puṇṇa sent a large sum of money to Uttarā who allowed her husband to spend a portion of it to enjoy the company of the courtezan, Sirimā, for a fortnight, and during this period she was freed from restraint and could offer charity to the Buddha and his disciples and listen to the Buddha's sermons. The Buddha with his disciples came there and held a religious discourse and Uttarā after listening to it, attained the second stage of sanctification while her husband, father-in-law, mother-in-law and Sirimā with five hundred gaṇikās who had thus an opportunity of listening to the discourses of the Master, attained the first stage. Shortly afterwards, Uttarā died and was reborn in the Tāvatiṁsa heaven where she related to Mahāmoggallāna the events of her past life, when asked. (Vimānavatthu commentary, pp. 62-74).

Sirimāvimāna.

When the Buddha was at Kalandakanivāpa in Veluvana near Rājagaha, Sirimā returned home after attaining the first stage of sanctification. In order to rid herself of sins, she used to offer alms to eight bhikkhus daily and every day she used to spend sixteen kahāpaṇas on works of charity. One day a bhikkhu accepted her offerings. As soon as he left, Sirimā fell ill and died. After death she was reborn as a celestial nymph who came to worship the Buddha with five hundred female attendants (Vimānavatthu commentary, p. 75 foll).

Kesakārivimāna.

When the Buddha was residing at Isipatana in Benares, some bhikkhus were going for alms by the gate of a Brahmin's house. A daughter of the brahmin named Kesakārī was picking up vermins from the head of her mother. The daughter seeing the bhikkhus asked her mother why they had renounced the world at an early age. The mother replied that they had done so after listening to the discourses of the Buddha. A lay disciple of the Buddha who was then passing by, heard the conversation, and explained to them the precepts of the Buddhist faith including the three refuges, the five precepts and the thirty-two impurities. The girl was attracted by these teachings and meditating on those impurities, attained the first stage and after death was reborn as an attendant of Sakka who when asked related the events of her past life. (Vimānavatthu commentary, pp. 86-89).

When the Buddha was at Jetavana at Sāvatthī, a lay disciple went to Jetavana in the evening and told the Buddha that from the next day he would offer charity to four bhikkhus daily. The Buddha having expressed his approval, arrangements were made in his house to offer charities daily to four bhikkhus and his maid servant was ordered to attend on the four bhikkhus daily, to prepare seats for them and supply water and other necessary things. The maid servant served the bhikkhus with hearty devotion and observed the precepts of the true dhamma and meditated on the thirty-two impurities for sixteen years, as a result of which she was reborn after death as one of the beloved attendants of Sakka. (Vimānavatthu commy. pp. 91-92).

Dāsīvimāna.

When the Lord was staying at Benares, there lived near one of the gates called the Kevaṭṭadvāra, a woman called Lakhumā. As the bhikkhus entered the town by that gate, she offered a spoonful of rice to the bhikkhus and thenceforth she imbibed the habit of offering charity and she used to prepare seats and supply water to the bhikkhus in the āsanasālā (rest house). She was established in sotāpatti and after death was reborn in the Tāvatiṁsa heaven. (Vimānavatthu commentary, pp. 97-98).

Lakhumāvimāna.

When the Buddha was at Kalandakanivāpa

Acāmadāyikāvimāna. at Veluvana, near Rājagaha, plague broke out in a family at Rājagaha and all the members died except one woman who fled from the house with her life. Helpless she took shelter behind a house the inmates of which gave her the remnants of their food including ācāma (scum of boiling rice). At that time Mahākassapa rising up from meditation, was moved by pity at the miserable plight of the woman and wishing to free her from the misery, he thought of giving her an opportunity of doing good deeds. Accordingly, the sage went to her and asked for alms and she offered him the ācāma. When approving her offering, he informed her that she had been his mother in the third previous existence. She died and was reborn among the Nimmānaratidevas. (Vimānavatthu commentary, pp. 100-101).

Caṇḍālīvimāna. When the Buddha was at Rājagaha, he came to know by meditation that a caṇḍālī whose death was very near, would fall into hell after death. Moved with pity to save her from the impending disaster, he went out for alms with a large gathering of bhikkhus and was passing by the spot where the caṇḍālī was. The caṇḍālī who was at that time walking with a stick seeing the Exalted One coming, stood by, looking towards him. He also, as if to prevent her proceeding on her way, stood in front of her and the sage Mahāmoggallāna exhorted the caṇḍālī to fall down at the feet of the Buddha and worship him in order to save herself from falling into hell, as her life was about to end. She with great devotion worshipped the Buddha who then left her for the town. The caṇḍālī was killed by a cow and after death she was reborn in the Tāvatiṁsa heaven. (Vimānavatthu commentary, pp. 105-107).

Bhadditthīvimānā.

When the Buddha was at Jetavana at Sāvatthī, there lived in the town of Kimbila, a householder's son named Rohaka who was a believer in the Buddha, and there was, in another family of equal status, in the same town, a girl, mild, gentle and devoted who, on account of her merits, was called Bhaddā. Rohaka married the girl Bhaddā who, on account of her good conduct, came to be known in that town as Bhadditthī or the gentle dame. At that time two of the most prominent among the disciples of the Buddha, in the course of their tour, came to the town of Kimbila. Rohaka invited the two disciples with their followers, offered them good food and drink and various other things and in company with his wife served them in every way and listening to their discourses, embraced the faith and received the five *sīlas*. Since then Bhaddā used to observe the Uposatha on the 8th, 14th and 15th day of every half month. On account of her piety, the gods used to help her and they even freed her from calumny. She after death was reborn in the Tāvatiṁsa heaven and she worshipped the Buddha when the Master went to the Tāvatiṁsa heaven (Vimānavatthu commentary, pp. 109-110).

Soṇadinnāvimāna.

When the Exalted One was at Sāvatthī, at Nālandā, there was a devoted upāsikā named Soṇadinnā who always used to serve the bhikkhus with the four requisites and also used to observe the precept and the uposatha with perfect regularity. She attained sotāpatti meditating on the four noble truths. She, after death, was reborn in the Tāvatiṁsa heaven. (Vimānavatthu commentary, p. 115).

Uposàthavimāna.

Uposatha, a devoted Upāsikā, in the city of Sāketa, used to observe like the lady in the above story, all the precepts, offered the four requisites to the bhikkhus and meditated on the four noble truths and thus attained sotāpatti. She after death was reborn in the Tāvatiṁsa heaven. (Vimānavatthu commentary, p. 115).

Exactly similar accounts are given of the two ladies of Rājagaha, Niddā and Suniddā who on account of their good conduct, were reborn in the Tāvatiṁsa heaven after their death.

Bhikkhādāyikavimāna.

When the Buddha was at Sāvatthī, a woman of Uttaramadhurā was at the end of her life-term and was about to fall into hell. Buddha seeing her miserable plight, took pity on her and came to save her. In the forenoon, Buddha proceeded towards her house for alms. The woman who was at that time coming with a pitcher of water, saw the Buddha and asked him whether he had received alms. The Buddha replied "I shall get it." She invited the Buddha to have his daily meal at her house. She gave a seat to the Buddha and fed him to his satisfaction with her own hands. She, after death, was reborn in the Tāvatiṁsa heaven. (Vimānavatthu commentary, pp. 118-119).

Ulāravimāna.

When the Buddha was at Veluvana, a girl of the family that supported Mahāmoggallāna's, was in the habit of offering charity to the bhikkhus. She used to give away in charity half the portion of the food that she received for herself and she never ate anything without giving a portion of it to others. Her mother used to give her double the quantity of food she would require for her own use in order to enable her to practise charity to her heart's content. The girl, when she grew up, was married to a young man of a family of false-believers. One day Mahāmoggallāna came and stood in front of her house in the course of his begging tour from house to house. The girl invited him to her house and offered him the cake which was reserved for her mother-in-law who, when she came to learn of it, grew angry and struck her on her shoulder. The girl died and after death was reborn in the Tāvatiṁsa heaven. (Vimānavatthu commentary, pp. 120-121).

Ucchudāyikavimāna.

The details of this vimāna are the same as those of the previous story except that the girl gave in charity to Mahāmoggallāna a piece of sugarcane reserved for her mother-in-law. (Vimānavatthu commentary, p. 124.)

Pallaṅkavimāna.

A daughter of an upāsaka at Sāvatthī was married to a member of another family of equal status. She was virtuous, free from anger, devoted to her husband and an observer of the sabbath. After death she was reborn in the Tāvatiṁsa heaven. (Vimānavatthu commentary, p. 128).

Latāvimāna.

While the Buddha was residing at Jetavana at Sāvatthī, an upāsaka of the city had a daughter named Latā who was learned, wise and intelligent. After marriage, she went to her father-in-law's house where she was faithful to her husband, and obedient to her father-in-law and mother-in-law and always used to speak sweet words to all the members of the family. She pleased every one in the family with food and drink, was capable of managing household affairs and also the property, was pious and free from anger, and was in the habit of giving charity and observing sabbath.

She, after death, was reborn as a daughter of Vessavana Kuvera named Latā and had four other sisters, Sajjā, Pavarā, Acchimatī and Sutā. All these five sisters were appointed dancing girls by Sakka. They afterwards grew jealous of each other and prayed to Vessavana to judge who amongst them was the most accomplished in the arts of dancing and music. Their father asked them to sing and dance in the assembly of the gods on the bank of the Anotatta lake. Latā was declared to be the best amongst the sisters. (Vimānavatthu commentary, pp. 131-132).

Guttilavimāna.

In very ancient times when Brahmadatta was reigning at Benares, the Bodhisatta was born there in the family of a musician. He was perfect in the art of music, became the chief musician in the Jambudīpa and was known as Guttila on account of his sweet voice. His parents were old and blind. Hearing of his great renown, a musician named Mūsila came to him from Ujjayinī to have lessons in the art of music from him. Guttila refused to take him as a pupil, noticing in his appearance marks of a wicked and ungrateful person. Mūsila, however, served Guttila's parents to their satisfaction and at last at the request of his parents, Guttila was persuaded to teach Mūsila and he taught the man all the secrets of the art without keeping back anything. Mūsila after acquiring the art from him, thought of defeating his teacher and with this end in view, he went to the King of Benares and demonstrated his skill in music. But it is to be noted that Guttila was the chief court musician of the king of Benares. Mūsila requested the king to appoint him as one of his musicians. The king agreed to appoint him on half the salary of Guttila. Mūsila, however, urged that he was in no way inferior to his teacher and demanded an equal salary. The king was requested to examine their skill in music and there was a competition in which Guttila with the help of Sakka proved to be superior. In the previous birth Sakka was a pupil of Guttila and he came to the assistance of his teacher who became victorious with his help and was requested to go to heaven, to give a performance of his skill in music before the gods. In Indra's Court he saw thirty-two heavenly nymphs possessing splendour greater than that of the other gods; and on account of various kinds of charity e.g. the offering of cloth, garland, perfume, fruit, sugarcane, etc., these nymphs had become liberated from earthly life. In heaven Guttila urged that he would not play on the vīṇā there without suitable remuneration and when asked what would satisfy him, he prayed that all those bright goddesses would recount to him the good deeds that had brought them to the heavenly regions. (Vimānavatthu commentary, pp. 137-148).

Daddalhavimāna.

When the Buddha was at Jetavana at Sāvatthī at Nālakagāma, one of the families that supported Revata had two daughters named Bhaddā and Subhaddā. Bhaddā went to her (Bhaddā's) husband's house. She was faithful and intelligent but barren. She requested her husband to marry her sister, a son by whom would be just like a son born of herself, and the family line would be continued thereby. Persuaded by her, the husband married Subhaddā who was always instructed by Bhaddā to offer charity, to observe the precepts and to perform other meritorious deeds diligently; so that, in consequence of this, Subhaddā would be happy in this world and in the next. Subhaddā acted according to her sister's advice and one day invited Revata. The thera, however, in order to secure comparatively great blessings for her, took it as an invitation to the Saṁgha and went to her house accompanied by eleven other bhikkhus and Subhaddā offered good food and drink to them. The thera approved of her charity and as a result of feeding the Saṁgha, she, after death, was reborn in the Nimmānarati heaven. When in heaven she looked for her sister who had made greater gifts than herself and found her in an inferior position, reborn as an attendant at the court of Sakka. She enquired about the reason of this difference in their respective position and learnt that Bhaddā had offered charity to individual bhikkhus and not to the Saṁgha, as had been done by herself and in consequence she was reborn as a nymph in Sakka's Court. (Vimānavatthu commentary, pp. 149-156).

Pesavatīvimāna.

When the Buddha was at Jetavana at Sāvatthī, there was at Nālakagāma in the country of Magadha, in the family of a householder, a daughter-in-law named Pesavatī. In a former birth when she was a young girl, she had once gone with her mother to a place where a stūpa was being built over the relic of Kassapa Buddha. There she had seen golden bricks being made and had offered her gold ornaments to be utilised for the erection of the stūpa. In consequence of this meritorious deed, after death, she was reborn in the devaloka and from that devaloka, she was reborn in the family of a householder at Nālakagāma at the time of the present Buddha. When twelve years old, she was sent by her mother to a shop to buy oil. She saw the son of the shop-keeper taking out his hidden treasure and throwing it away. Sinful as he was, he could not appreciate the value of the treasure which appeared to him to be worthless stone but she being virtuous recognised the true worth of the treasure and she asked the shopkeeper why the treasure was being thrown away. The shopkeeper, thinking that she was virtuous and that if he could marry his son to her, his hidden treasure might be saved, went to the parents of the girl and sought the hand of the girl for his son. She was then married to the shopkeeper's son and the shopkeeper made her the mistress of the house, placed her in charge of the treasure-vault and called her Pesavatī. Her virtues enabled them to enjoy the rich treasure there. At that time Sāriputta obtained parinibbāṇa at Nālakagāma. Pesavatī showed her respect to the dead body of Sāriputta by worshipping it with sweet scents, flowers, etc. In the crowd assembled there, a great panic was created by the royal elephant having run amok and in the stampede that followed, Pesavatī was crushed to death. As at the moment of death, her mind was full of respect and devotion to Sāriputta she was reborn in the Tāvatiṁsa heaven. (Vimānavatthu commentary, pp. 156-159).

Mallikāvimāna.

While the Exalted One had attained mahāparinibbāṇa at Kusīnārā and while gods and men vied with one another in doing reverence to the body of the Buddha, Mallikā, the wife of Bandhula and the daughter of a Malla king of Kusīnārā, offered worship to the relic of the Buddha with a plenty of perfumes and garlands and also an ornament named Mahālatā which was very valuable. In consequence of this, she, after death, was reborn in the Tāvatiṁsa heaven, where she was bedecked in all yellow. (Vimānavatthu commentary, p. 165).

Visālakkhīvimāna.

After the Buddha's parinibbāṇa, King Ajātasattu erected a stūpa over the relic of the Buddha that fell to his share. A daughter of a garland-maker of Rājagaha, Sunandā by name, daily used to send to the stūpa garlands, perfumes, fruits, flowers, etc., for the worship of the relic and on the uposatha day, she used to offer worship herself with her own hands at the stūpa. After death, she was reborn as an attendant of Sakka, who, on one occasion, addressed her as Visālakkhī. (Vimānavatthu commentary, pp. 169-170).

Pāricchattakavimāna

When the Buddha was at Sāvatthī, an upāsaka of the city invited the Buddha to his house and in front of the gate of his residence, he erected a beautiful pandal, and prepared nice and costly seats for the Buddha and his disciples. He offered excellent food, drink, garlands and perfumes to the Buddha. At that time a woman went to collect fire-wood at Andhavana and while returning home, with a large bundle of asoka twigs, with young leaves and beautiful flowers on them, she saw the Buddha seated in the pandal and worshipped him with asoka flowers brought from that forest. She twice went round the Buddha to show her respect towards him, then bowed and went her way. In consequence of this meritorious deed, she, after death, was reborn in the Tāvatiṁsa heaven having a thousand apsarases to attend on her and passed her time sporting, dancing and weaving heavenly garlands in the garden of Nandana. (Vimānavatthu commentary, p. 173).

Mañjeṭṭhakavimāna.

When the Buddha was at Jetavana, an upāsaka invited him to dinner at his residence, erected a pandal in front of the gate of the house, and provided beautiful seats. At that time a maid-servant of another family came to the spot with many sāla flowers collected from the Andhavana; with them she worshipped the Buddha, thrice went round him and after making her obeisance, went away. After death she was reborn in the Tāvatiṁsa heaven and got a red glass palace fronted with a sāla garden. (Vimānavatthu commentary, pp. 176-177).

Pabhassaravimāna.

When the Buddha was residing at Rājagaha, an upāsaka of that city was very much devoted to Mahāmoggallāna. The upāsaka's daughter was also devoted to him. One day Mahāmoggallāna, while on his usual round for alms, went to the upāsaka's place and the daughter welcomed him, offered him a seat, worshipped him with a garland of sumana flower and gave him sweets, etc. The thera was waiting to approve of her charity but she told him that as she too had many duties at home, she would listen to his religious discourse another day. She died on that day as her life-period was over. She after death was reborn in the

Tāvatiṁsa heaven. (Vimānavatthu commentary, pp. 178-179).

Nāgavimāna.

An upāsikā of Benares was very much devoted to the Buddha. She got a pair of clothes woven, washed them with great care and offered them to the Lord. The latter accepted the present and delivered a religious discourse to her. In consequence of this good deed, she, after death, was reborn in the Tāvatiṁsa heaven, became the beloved of Sakka, acquired the name of Yasuttarā and received there an elephant decorated with golden ornaments. (Vimānavatthu commentary, pp. 181-182).

Alomavimāna.

When the Buddha was at Sārnātha in Benares, one forenoon he went out for alms and entered the city. A poor woman named Alomā not finding anything better to offer, presented some rotten cooked rice without salt to the Buddha who accepted it. In consequence of this good deed, she, after death, was reborn in the Tāvatiṁsa heaven. (Vimānavatthu commentary, p. 184).

Kañjikadāyika-vimāna.

When the Buddha was at Andhakavinda, he once had pain in his stomach. He told Ānanda to go for alms and he was instructed to bring Kañjika or fermented rice gruel, if offered. Ānanda went to the house of the Buddha's physician, and on the wife of the physician asking him about the medicine, Ānanda told her that he was in need of rice gruel. The lady filled with respect for the Buddha, prepared a medicated drink of rice-gruel and filling the begging bowl with it, offered it to Ānanda knowing that this was required for the Buddha. Besides the rice-gruel, she also offered nice food and drink. The Buddha was relieved of his pain after taking the gruel. The woman, after death, was reborn in the Tāvatiṁsa heaven and enjoyed there various kinds of heavenly pleasures. (V. commentary, 185-186).

Vihāravimāna.

The Buddha was at Jetavana. On a festival day, Visākhā, the great upāsikā of Sāvatthī, went out decked in all her rich apparel and ornaments specially the mahālatā, an ornament of extraordinary beauty and of immense value, intending to spend the day in the city-garden with her maids and attendants. But on the way the idea struck her, "Why am I thus going out like a mere girl, what have I got to do with such worthless sports? I had better repair to the vihāra and listen to the noble discourses of the Lord." Moved by this thought and unwilling to waste her time idly she went to the vihāra where the Buddha was residing. There the lady took off the Mahālatā ornament and gave it to her maid-servant to keep it while she would be listening to the religious discourse. Coming out of the vihāra she asked for her ornament after she had walked some distance from the place.

The maid-servant told her that she had left it by mistake at the vihāra and offered to go and bring it back. But Visākhā with her maid-servant returned to the vihāra saying that if it was in the vihāra, she would not take it back. She offered it to the Buddha and under his directions, she built a vihāra with the sale proceeds of the ornament, which amounted to nine krores and a lac. Visākhā offered to her maid-servant all the merit that accrued for constructing the vihāra. The latter approved of her charity and died shortly afterwards. After death, she was reborn in the Tāvatiṁsa heaven and she received in heaven a glorious vimāna surrounded by gardens, tanks and many objects of beauty and comfort. But Visākhā on account of her boundless charity, was born in the Nimmānarati heaven and became the chief queen of Sunimmita, king of that heaven. (Vimānavatthu commentary, pp. 187-189).

Caturitthivimāna.

Mahāmoggallāna saw in the Tāvatiṁsa heaven four celestial nymphs in four vimānas each surrounded by a thousand attendants, and asked them to relate the good deeds that had brought them there. They said that they had lived at the time of Kassapa Buddha in the kingdom of Esikā and in the city of Punnakata. When of age they got married and lived in their husbands' house. One of the nymphs added that in consequence of her giving a bunch of indīvara flowers to a bhikkhu, she was reborn as a celestial nymph. Another said that in consequence of her giving a blue lotus to a bhikkhu, she was reborn as a nymph. The third nymph offered a lotus to a bhikkhu and so she attained the state of a heavenly nymph. The fourth woman gave blossoms of sumana flowers to a bhikkhu and thus acquired the state of a celestial nymph. At the time of Gautama Buddha, they were in heaven and were met there by Mahāmoggallāna who, after listening to their talk, delivered a religious discourse to them who then reached the first stage of sanctification (Vimānavatthu commentary, pp. 195-196).

Ambavimāna.

When the Buddha was at Sāvatthī, an upāsikā after realising the great merit of offering a hermitage to the Buddha and his pupils, asked the permission of the Buddha to build a hermitage and to offer it to him. She obtained the permission and built a beautiful hermitage with groves of mango trees all round, decorated also with flower-gardens and other things so that it looked a very beautiful and splendid place to live in. She then covered all the trees with rich clothes, lighted innumerable lights and offered it to the Buddha and his followers. In consequence of this meritorious deed she was reborn in the Tāvatiṁsa heaven where she got a splendid vimāna surrounded by mango gardens. (Vimānavatthu commentary, p. 198).

Ajātasattu built a stūpa over the relics of the

Pītavimāna

body of the Buddha. Early in the morning, an upāsikā of Rājagaha after purifying herself in the bath, was going to worship the stūpa with four Kosātakī flowers. On the way she was killed by a milch cow with a new born calf. After death, she was reborn in the Tāvatiṁsa heaven and appeared before Sakka when he was enjoying himself in the heavenly gardens. (Vimānavatthu commentary, p. 200).

Vandanavimāna.

When the Buddha was at Sāvatthī, many bhikkhus after spending the rainy season in a village hermitage, were going to Sāvatthī to worship the Buddha and, on their way, they passed through another village. A woman of the village, seeing them was filled with veneration and after making obeisance to them, stood watching them with great respect and devotion, till they were out of sight. After death, she was reborn in the Tāvatiṁsa heaven. (Vimānavatthu commentary, p. 205).

Rajjumālāvimāna.

A daughter of a Brahmin at Gayāgāma became the mistress of her father-in-law's house. She disliked a maidservant's daughter, whom she hated and used to beat for fault or no fault of hers. Even when the maid's daughter came of age, there was no remission of the kicks and blows which became all the more severe as days went on. The fact was that at the time of Kassapa Buddha the girl had been the mistress and she used to ill-treat and beat her maid who was now born as the Brāhmaṇa lady and the situation was reversed.

The mistress used to punish the maid servant's daughter by pulling the hair of her head, the maid-servant's daughter, therefore, had the hair of her head shaved by a barber. The mistress tied her head with a rope and punished her and thus the girl came to be called Rajjumālā. At last she went to a forest to commit suicide, unable any more to bear the rude treatment of the mistress. There she saw the Buddha sitting at the foot of a tree. She listened to his religious discourse. The master of the house coming to know of it, invited the Buddha to his house and his presence changed the mind also of his daughter-in-law who thenceforth came to like the girl whom she had hated before and ceased to ill-treat her. In consequence of her meritorious deed, the servant-girl, after death, was reborn in the Tāvatiṁsa heaven. (Vimānavatthu commy. pp. 206-209.)

Maṇḍūkadevaputta-vimāna.

When the Buddha was at Campā on the bank of the famous tank, Gaggarā, he went out for alms and after returning home, one evening he gave religious instruction to the bhikkhus in an enchanting voice that charmed even the lower animals. At this time a frog came out of the Gaggarā tank and listened to the voice of the Buddha with great pleasure. As the frog listened entranced to the Lord's voice it was trod upon by a cow-herd who also had been attracted by the discourse. The frog died and in consequence of its meritorious deed, it was at once reborn in the Tāvatiṁsa heaven and there becoming conscious of all that had happened, came down in its heavenly chariot to the place where the discourse was going on, with the purpose of worshipping the Buddha. (Vimānavatthu commentary, pp. 217-218).

Revatīvimāna.

Revatī was the wife of Nandiya, a householder's son at Sārnāth. At first she was very unfaithful, uncharitable and impious. Afterwards being instructed by Nandiya, she used to offer charity to please him but when he was absent from home, she stopped all gifts and offerings and also when Nandiya died, she reverted to her evil practices, spoke all sorts of lies about the bhikkhus and stopped all works of charity that her husband had instituted. The result was that while enjoying the blessings of the Tāvatiṁsa heaven, Revatī was taken from one hell to another to suffer for her misdeeds (Vimānavatthu commentary, pp. 220 foll).

Chattamāṇavaka-vimāna.

Chatta was the son of a Brahmin at Setabba. His father sent him for education to a renowned teacher Pokkharasāti at Ukkaṭṭhā. He was intelligent and diligent and soon acquired a knowledge of the

Brahmanical lore. At his prayer, the teacher asked him to bring one thousand kahāpaṇas as the teacher's fee. He went home and his parents procured the money for him and he was to start with it on the morrow. Robbers coming to know of this decided to waylay him. The Buddha by his powers coming to know of his impending death, set out from the vihāra in the early dawn and meeting him on the way converted him to the faith. Proceeding on his way he met the robbers while passing through a forest and was killed. For his devotion to the faith he was reborn in the Tāvatiṁsa heaven and was rewarded with a splendid vimāna known as Chattavimāna after him. (V. commentary, pp. 229-33).

Kakkaṭakarasadāyaka-vimāna

When the Buddha was at Rājagaha at Veluvana, there was a bhikkhu who used to make very strenuous efforts to meditate on vipassanākammaṭṭhāna. The Bhikkhu suffered from acute pain in the ear and could not get rid of it in spite of the best medical help. He informed the Buddha of his difficulty and the Buddha knowing that the soup prepared from the crab was the best medicine for his disease, asked him to go to Magadha for alms. Here he stood in front of a hut of a farmer who had got ready for his own meal rice and crab soup which he offered to the bhikkhu. The bhikkhu was at once relieved of his pain, became very happy and even before his dinner was finished, he reached the stage of an arahat. Moved with gratitude he heartily blessed the farmer who, after death, was reborn in the Tāvatiṁsa heaven having a vimāna with a golden crab hung in front of it. (Vimānavatthu commentary, pp. 243-244).

Dvārapālakavimāna.

An upāsaka of Rājagaha daily used to offer food to four bhikkhus. But there being some thieves in the neighbourhood of his house, the door of his house had always to be kept closed for fear of robbery, and on account of this, the bhikkhus had sometimes to return empty-handed from his house. Once he asked his wife whether offerings were regularly made to the bhikkhus. He was told that for some days the bhikkhus had not turned up for alms, perhaps because the doors were closed. The householder appointed a gate-keeper to receive the bhikkhus when they approached his house for alms. The gatekeeper used to do his duty with care and devotion and by listening to the exhortations of the bhikkhus, he was converted to the faith. The upāsaka, after death, was reborn in the Yāma heaven and the door-keeper who used to welcome the bhikkhus, was reborn in the Tāvatiṁsa heaven after death. (Vimānavatthu commentary, pp. 246-247).

Karaṇiyavimāna.

When the Buddha was at Sāvatthī, an upāsaka while returning from the river Aciravatī after taking his bath, saw the Buddha going for alms. Learning on enquiry that the Buddha had not till then been invited by anybody, he with great veneration besought the Buddha to favour him by taking his dinner at his house. He then led the Buddha to his residence and placed excellent food and drink before him. After death, he was reborn in the Tāvatiṁsa heaven. (V. commy. p. 248).

Sūcivimāna.

When the Exalted One was at Rājagaha at Veluvana, Sāriputta required a needle to sew his garment. He, on his needle-begging tour, came to the house of a blacksmith who, coming to know of his need, offered him two new needles for his use and requested him to come to his house whenever in future there was need of any like object. Sāriputta blessed him for his good intention and by virtue of this good deed, after death, the blacksmith was reborn in the Tāvatiṁsa heaven. (Vimānavatthu commentary, p. 250).

Dutiya-sūcivimāna.

A bhikkhu was in need of a needle at a vihāra at Veluvana at Rājagaha. A tailor who had gone to the vihāra on a visit, coming to know of his need, offered some needles to the bhikkhu who blessed him. After death, the tailor was reborn in the Tāvatiṁsa heaven. (Vimānavatthu commentary, p. 251).

Mahāmoggallāna saw in heaven a devaputta

Nāgavimāna.

mounted on an all-white elephant and attended by a large retinue and asked him what he had done in his previous life to earn them. The Devaputta replied that he had placed with his own hands eight mutta flowers at the stūpa built over the relic of Kassapa Buddha's body. It appears that at that time, Kikī, the King of Kāsī, with his nobles and the citizens of his capital, used to offer heaps of flowers at the golden stūpa of Kassapa Buddha, so that flowers became very rare and could be had at a high price. The above upāsaka obtained with much difficulty only eight flowers from a florist and with them he worshipped the stūpa. In consequence of this good deed, he was reborn as a devaputta in various vimānas and came to the Tāvatiṁsa heaven at the time of the Buddha Gautama. (V. commentary, pp. 252-54)

Dutiyanāgavimāna.

An upāsaka of Rājagaha was faithful, charitable, and was established in the three refuges and the five *sīlas*. In the morning he used to offer alms to various bhikkhus, in the afternoon he used to go to the vihāra with offerings of various sweet drinks and used to listen to religious discourses. After death, he was reborn in the Tāvatiṁsa heaven, possessing an all-white elephant. One day he came to the Veluvana with his vimāna (chariot) to worship the Buddha. (V. commy. 254-255).

While the Buddha was at Rājagaha, three

Tatiyanāgavimāna. bhikkhus, after their rainy-weather-sojourn, were coming there from a distant village to pay their respects to him. But as night overtook them on the way, they repaired to a sugar-cane field, the keeper of which repuested them to stay there for the night. No houses being available there, the man prepared a cot with sugarcane stalks and upon it made a bed of sugarcane leaves for one bhikkhu; similarly he prepared cots and beds of straw and cloth for the other two bhikkhus. Next morning, when the bhikkhus were ready to start on their journey, he offered them rice with sugarcane juice and also a piece of sugarcane to each of them. A Brahmin who was a false believer and was the owner of the field, met the bhikkhus on the way and coming to learn from them that his servant had been so very liberal with his sugarcane, flew into a rage with the field-keeper and beat him to death. After death the man was born in the Mote-Hall called Sudhamma of the gods. (V. commentary, pp. 255-257).

Cūlarathavimāna. After the Buddha's parinibbāṇa, Mahākaccāyana used to live in a forest-hermitage in a frontier province. At that time, in the kingdom of Assaka a king named Assaka ruled in the city of Potana; Sujāta, the son of his first wife, was banished at the importunate insistence of his younger wife. Sujāta took up his residence in the same forest where

Mahākaccāyana was living. A god who was Sujāta's well-wisher, came to him in the guise of a deer. Sujāta followed the deer with the intention of capturing it and the deer disappeared near the hermitage of Mahākaccāyana. Mahākaccāyana instructed him in the faith and as he found that the young prince had only five months to live, advised him to go to his father and perform meritorious deeds during the short period of life that was still remaining. Sujāta, at his behest, went to the city, took up his residence in the city gardens and informed his father of his return. He explained to his father how he had a short period to live and with his help built a vihāra and then invited the thera to come there. The king cordially welcomed him and Sujāta performing more meritorious deeds, was, after death, reborn in the Tāvatiṁsa heaven and he got a chariot decorated with seven kinds of gems, and seven yojanas in extent. (Vimānavatthu commentary, 259-270).

Mahārathavimāna.

A devaputta named Gopāla of Tāvatiṁsa heaven worshipped in a previous birth the Buddha Vipassi with a garland of gold, in order that he might have a golden garland hanging from his neck in all his births. He passed through many births enjoying the object of his desire. At the time of Kassapa Buddha, he was reborn as the son of King Kikī of Benares and made immense gifts and received the dhamma from that Buddha, but failing to reach the higher stages he was again reborn in the Tāvatiṁsa heaven. He enjoyed the blessings of the various heavens for a long time and at the time of Buddha Gautama, he was found in the Tāvatiṁsa heaven by Mahāmoggallāna. The great thera coming to learn of his previous births, again explained to him the principles of the faith, and Gopāla became established in the Sotāpatti stage. (V. commy. 270-271).

Agāriyavimāna.

A rich couple of Rājagaha were pious and charitable and the door of their house was open to bhikkhus and bhikkhuṇīs, many of whom were supported by them. Both husband and wife performed various meritorious deeds for the three refuges throughout their life and in consequence, they were reborn in the Tāvatiṁsa heaven, having very large golden vimāna full of celestial comforts. (Vimānavatthu commentary, p. 286).

Phaladāyakavimāna.

When the Exalted One was residing at Rājagaha, King Bimbisāra had once the desire to have mangoes out of season. The gardener was asked to get mangoes but he requested the King to wait a few days during which he would take steps to make the trees yield fruits, as that was not the proper season. The gardener caused the mango trees to bear fruits out of season and was going to the king with four mangoes when he met Mahāmoggallāna who was out for alms. He gave them to Mahāmoggallāna thinking that such an act of charity would do him good in this world and the next. He came to the king and related the matter. The king sent men to make enquiries about the truth of the statement and they reported that the Thera had presented the mangoes to the Buddha who again had given one mango to each of Sāriputta, Mahāmoggallāna and Mahākassapa and had eaten the fourth himself. The king thought very highly of the gardener who even at the risk of his life had been moved to perform such an act of charity, and presented the gardener with one village, various kinds of clothes and ornaments, etc., and asked him to make over to him (the king) a portion of the merit acquired by the gift of the mangoes. The gardener did so and after death, was reborn in the Tāvatiṁsa heaven. (Vimānavatthu commentary, pp. 288-289).

Upassayadāyaka-vimāna.

A bhikkhu who had passed the rainy season in a village-hermitage near Rājagaha, was going to Veluvana to worship the Buddha. In the evening he found himself in another village and meeting there an upāsaka he enquired whether there was any place where monks could spend the night. The upāsaka took him to his own house and after consulting his wife cordially received him and gave one room to the bhikkhu. The next-day he requested the bhikkhu to accept food and after feeding him to his satisfaction, gave him a lump of jaggarie with which to prepare a drink on the way. He accompanied the bhikkhu some distance out of his village and came back. The upāsaka with his wife, after death, was reborn in the Tāvatiṁsa heaven. (V. commy. p. 291).

Bhikkhādāyaka-vimāna.

A bhikkhu of Rājagaha going about for alms stood before the door of a householder. An inmate of that house, who after having washed his hands and feet, had placed his food on a dish and was just going to partake of it, saw the bhikkhu and at once offered his own food to the bhikkhu who accepted the food and blessed him. In consequence of this good deed, he, after death, was reborn in the Tāvatiṁsa heaven. (Vimānavatthu commentary, pp. 292-293).

Yavapālakavimāna.

A poor boy of Rājagaha was appointed to guard the barley field of some person. One day in the morning his master gave him for breakfast some kummāsa (i.e. sour gruel) and sent him to look after the field. He took the food to the field and sat down at the foot of a tree in order to partake of it and at that moment an arahant wandering for alms came there and sat down at the foot of the same tree. The boy on enquiry coming to learn that the bhikkhu had not had any food till then, offered his own food to him, which he accepted and blessed him. The poor boy after death, was reborn in the Tāvatiṁsa heaven. (Vimānavatthu commentary, p. 294).

Kuṇḍalīvimāna.

The Exalted One was residing at Sāvatthī. At that time two of the chief disciples of the Buddha with their attendants were touring the country of Kāsī and in the course of their wanderings, came to a vihāra in the evening. Coming to learn of their arrival, an upāsaka of a neighbouring village came there and made arrangements for their stay at night and invited them to take their food in his house next morning. He offered plenty of excellent food and drink to them at his house next morning and the upāsaka after death, was reborn in the Tāvatiṁsa heaven. (Vimānavatthu commentary, p. 295).

Uttaravimāna.

After the parinibbāṇa of the Buddha, when the relics of his body had been placed in the stūpas at various places and when the great saṅgīti was taking place, among the bhikkhus who were requested to attend the First Council, the sage Kumārakassapa with five hundred bhikkhus, spent the rainy season in a certain forest of sinisapā trees near Setabba city. King Pāyāsi with his retinue went to him and the thera wishing to expound to him the continuity of life after death, delivered before him the excellent Pāyāsi-sutta which is full of the most convincing arguments, instructed him in the dhamma and converted him to the Buddhist faith. The king after conversion, practised charity but on a rather poor scale, not worthy of his position. In consequence of this miserly charity, he, after death, was rewarded with a position in a comparatively low heaven, in the Cātummahārājikadevaloka. An officer of King Pāyāsi called Uttara, had spent all his wealth in acts of charity and used to perform meritorious deeds, with great devotion. In consequence he, after death, was reborn in the Tāvatiṁsa heaven. (Vimānavatthu commentary, pp. 297-298).

Cittalatāvimāna.

While the Buddha was at Sāvatthī, a poor man of the city used to earn his bread by serving other people. He was very faithful, devoted to the three gems and was obedient to his parents. He did not marry, thinking that the women who came to live with their husbands did not treat their fathers-in-law and mothers-in-law with proper respect and devotion such as he himself used to show to his parents. He after death was reborn in the Tāvatiṁsa heaven. (Vimānavatthu commentary, p. 299).

Maṇithūṇavimāna.

When the Lord was residing at Jetavana near Sāvatthī, a laıge number of bhikkhus used to live in forest-hermitages. An upāsaka would sweep the path which the bhikkhus used when going out for alms. He used to level the roads, remove thorns, construct bridges over water course, dig tanks along the path and construct ghats or watering places for the bhikkhus. In every way he sought to make their journeys comfortable. He used to observe the precepts and offer charity. He after death was reborn in the Tāvatiṁsa heaven and his vimanā was marked out by beautiful maṇithūṇas or pillars of the costliest jewels. (V. commy., p. 301).

Suvaṇṇavimana.

When the Buddha was dwelling at Andhakavinda, an upāsaka who was faithful and very rich, built an excellent gandhakūṭi, provided with all necessary comforts, on a hillock at a little distance from the village and offered it to the Buddha whom he served there with great devotion. In consequence after death he was reborn in the Tāvatiṁsa heaven. (Vimānavatthu commy. p. 302).

Ambavimāna.

A poor man was the servant of a person who had set him to guard his mango garden. One day, in summer, Sāriputta who was passing by that garden became tired and exhausted and was perspiring profusely owing to the heat. The poor guard, out of devotion to him, requested him to come to the garden and take rest. He also brought water from a well for bathing and drinking. The thera after bathing and drinking, blessed him and went away. The garden-keeper, after death, was reborn in the Tāvatiṃsa heaven. (Vimānavatthu commentary, 305-306).

Gopālavimāna.

A gopāla (cowherd) of Rājagaha took with him to the field kummāsa or sour gruel for his breakfast. Mahāmoggallāna came to know that the poor cowherd would soon die and that if he would offer him the sour gruel, he would go to heaven. He came there out of pity, to give the gopāla an opportunity of saving himself; the cowherd who was about to eat the sour gruel offered it to him and then went away to drive out the cows from a coınfield they had entered. He was bitten by a snake on the way and coming back to the thera, he found the latter eating the sour grain and was pleased at the sight. Very soon the poison worked on him and after death he was reborn in the Tāvatiṁsa heaven. (V. commy. p. 308).

Kaṇṭhakavimāna.

In the night of the great renunciation, when the Bodhisatta said addressing his horse, Kaṇṭhaka, "Carry me, my darling and attaining *sambodhi* I shall deliver the world." Then the horse inspired with the consciousness of carrying that great burden on his back, was filled with immense joy and devotion. Again when on the bank of the river Anomā the Bodhisatta asked Kaṇṭhaka to return with Channa to Kapilavastu, the horse was weighed down with sorrow and licked the Bodhisatta's feet, and his heart was filled with noble ardour and devotion. In consequence of this, after death, the horse was reborn in the Tāvatiṁsa heaven and known as Kaṇṭhakadevaputta who one day while going to the Nandanavana in a celestial chariot, met Mahāmoggallāna on the way and related to him the events of his past life. (Vimānavatthu commentary, pp. 312-314).

Anekavaṇṇavimāna.

Thirty thousand kappas ago when Sumedha the sammāsambuddha, had attained mahāparinibbāṇa, and many caityas had been built over the relics of his body, a bhikkhu after leading the life of a celibate for a long time, again became a householder; but he was in the habit of performing meritorious deeds and he used to worship the caityas and listen to the discourses. After death he reached heaven and owing to the accumulation of much merit, he was more powerful than Sakka. In the deva and manussalokas, after various births, owing to the residue of his merit, at the time of Gautama Buddha, he was reborn in the Tāvatiṁsa heaven in a vimāna of diverse colours, that is, an anekavaṇṇavimāna, and was called as such by the other devaputtas. (Vimānavatthu commentary, 319-320).

Maṭṭhakuṇḍalīvimāna.

(See my work, The Buddhist Conception of Spirits, pp. 32-33).

Serīsakavimāna.

We have seen before in another vimāna story that King Pāyāsi of the city of Setavya was converted by the sage Kumāra-Kassapa, but he was not a liberal minded man and his acts of charity were done neither with a whole heart nor with his own hands. In consequence he, after death, could not reach the Tāvatiṁsa heaven but was reborn in the lower heaven of the Cātummahārājikas, in a vacant vimāna called the Serīsakavimāna. It had been built for a man who while living at the time of Kassapa-Buddha, had served a bhikkhu who was seated in the sun with a shade over him made with the branches of a Sirīsa tree bound together and lowered down. He after death was born in this vimāna which was marked out by a sirīsa forest in front of it and his vimāna was always decorated with sirīsa flowers. This man at the time of Gautama Buddha, was born on earth and reached the stage of an arahat ; he meeting the king in his deserted vimāna, asked him about his past history and coming to learn of it, preached to men how king Pāyāsi could not reach the higher heavens for not practising charity with his own hands. Vessavana Mahārāja placed the Serīsa-vimāna with the king in a desert for the shelter of travellers going through that desert. There he met a company of merchants of Aṅga and Magadha, who had lost their way in the desert. There was a long conversation between Pāyāsi and the merchants and at last he conveyed the merchants to Pāṭaliputta in his vimāna. One of the merchants named Saṁbhava was a religious upāsaka and he reported the whole conversation to the Theras and at the second saṅgīti, it was embodied in the compilation of the holy literature. (Vimānavatthu commy. pp. 331 foll).

Sunikkhittavimāna.

When Kassapa-Sammāsaṁbuddha had attained parinibbāṇa and an extensive *Kanaka-thūpa* was built over the relics of his body, large concourse of men used to come there to worship with flowers and perfumes. An upāsaka who was very much devoted to the worship of that Buddha, used to arrange properly the flowers scattered by the people, so that they looked beautiful and roused the ardour and devotion of men who visited the shrine. After doing this, he thought of the glories of the Buddha and felt a joy within himself and after death was reborn in a golden mansion in the Tāvatiṁsa heaven. (Vimānavatthu commentary, pp. 352 foll).

SECTION III

Observations

The form of the vimāna and its comforts proportionate to meritorious deeds.

It will be seen from the above account of the vimānas or celestial mansions that the form of the vimāna and the comforts and pleasures provided therein are proportionate not only to the meritorious deeds done on earth, but also to the particular nature of the deeds themselves, as also to the desire of the dweller of the vimāna. The girl of Rājagaha whose story is recorded in the Kuñjaravimāna was told by the learned, "Good lady, good deeds are like the Cintāmaṇi, the jewel with miraculous powers, which turns everything that it touches into gold, and they are also like the *Kapparukkha* or the divine tree that produces everything that one may desire from it. When the proper environment and the proper mental condition are produced, whatever one prays for when doing a work is sure to be won. By giving a seat one gets a very high position, by bestowing food one secures health and wealth, by the gift of clothes one acquires good complexion (vaṇṇa) and property; the gift of conveyances procures for the giver special happiness, and that of lights begets powers of vision; by giving a house one gets all sorts of property." (Vimānavatthu commentary, p. 32).

It appears from the stories given in the Vimānavatthu commentary that most of the departed spirits go to the Tāvatimsa heaven. Only in very rare cases do we read of a spirit passing to the regions of the higher gods, the Nimmānaratis. It is only in very exceptional cases indeed that spirits go to the Brahmaloka. Downward also we read only in one case, that of king Pāyāsi, that the King went to the region of Cātummahārājikadevas for stinginess in making gifts. His story also makes it clear that it is not the quantity but the devotion with which the gift is made, that determines the place one is to acquire after death.

The Tāvatiṁsa heaven —the abode of most of the departed spirits

Another thing that deserves notice is that the vimāna may not always be in the heavenly regions. As in the case of king Pāyāsi, the vimāna with its comforts was placed down below on earth in the midst of a desert. In the stories of the Petavatthu we have seen many such spirits living in their vimānas in solitary places on earth, on the sea, in the forest or amidst the sands of the desert. This is specially the case with the spirits in the lower heavens, who are not sufficiently purified or whose attachment to things on earth is still rather keen. The spirits could at will come down on earth in their vimānas, and in several cases they came to the Buddha on their vimānas

Location of the vimānas.

to listen to his discourse. Evidently these vimānas could not carry their occupants to the higher heavens; nowhere do we read of their going to any region higher than their own.

The heaven of the Buddhists is the heaven of a people with refined and delicate tendencies; it has nothing in common with the Valhalla where the spirits of the departed warriors, the worshippers of Odin and Thor, enjoy the supreme bliss of fighting and feasting. The fortunate dwellers in the Buddhist vimānas are marked out by a beautiful golden yellow complexion emitting rays of brilliance that make up a sort of aureole round about them. There is a play of brilliance and charming colours in the dress and in the paraphernalia in general of the dwellers in the heavenly palaces; all the wealth of India, gold and precious stones, rubies and sapphires, emeralds and diamonds abound in the vimānas. There are sweet-scented perfumes and an abundance of flowers, the padma, the utpala, the puṇḍarīka—all varieties of the lotus and the lily, the sirīsa, the campaka—in fact all the wealth of Indian flora. Beautiful plants and creepers, sometimes ujjānas or gardens and even huge trees—an *ambavana* as in the case of the Ambavimāna—beautify and lend grace to these palatial abodes of the Buddhist heaven. Out of these vimānas, in which there are dancing and music, come out

Dwellers in the Buddhist vimānas—their joys and comforts.

sweet sounds that enrapture the soul and regale the ears. (dibbā saddā nissaranti savaniyā manoramā). Soft breezes laden with perfumes come from them and fill the surrounding atmosphere. Garlands of the sweetest and most charming flowers worn on the head or hung from the neck bedeck the persons of the occupants of the vimānas, who have the human form but are far more brilliant and dazzling than an thing ever found on earth. We read of the *Chattamānavaka* that the sun in the heavens shines not so brilliant, nor is the moon so soft as the rays emitted by him. The sun's rays are pale in splendour before the dazzling brilliance of the vimāna, a brilliance that illumines twenty-five yojanas on all sides, and turns even the night into day. Some of the vimānas, like the Mahā rathavimāna of Gopāladevaputta, are drawn by a thousand horses. Twenty-four verses describe the beauties and splendour of this great chariot-like vimāna. We also read that this chariot like many others is painted in beautiful colours.

The pleasures of the Tāvatiṁsa heaven.

The pleasures enjoyed by the Tāvatiṁsa gods are mainly, if not entirely, physical; there is nothing of the deeper joys that enrapture the soul. The joys of the vimānas are inferior to the nobler and the purer bliss that is enjoyed by the pure soul, by the bhikkhu who holds the mere pleasures of the senses in absolute contempt. A bhikkhu who by restraint and freedom from desires acquired the stage of an Arahat, has no reason to be envious of these vimāna gods ; he is superior even to Sakka, the king of the Tāvatiṁsa gods. Even Brahmā is in no way superior to him. For the aspirant after the highest stages of *arahatta* and *nibbāṇa*, *puñña* and *pāpa* (merit and demerit) are equally reprehensible. The highest of the pleasures that these heavens bestow has a limit : it is not everlasting. When the fruits of a good deed are consumed, the man has again to come down to earth, to be buffetted by the waves of *kamma*, of *puñña* and *pāpa*. They can never bring about a final release from evil and hence, the experiences in heaven, though pleasurable, are an evil to be guarded against—the more so on account of their luring attractiveness.

The various grades of heaven.

The six heavens from the world of the Cātummahārājikadevas up to that of the Paranimmitavasavattīs are worlds of sensuous enjoyment or of sense experiences, the *Kāmalokas*, the worlds of desire or the heavens of the concupiscence-world. Beyond the Cātumahārājikadevas lies the world of the Tāvatimsa devas where, as we have seen, repair after death most of the ordinary mortals who have done some good deeds on earth, people who have done some good to the members of the saṁgha but have not entered the saṁgha proper, or if they have not entered even the first stage of the dhyāna, or meditation. Beyond the Tāvatiṁsa world, is the region of the Yāma or 'the misery-freed gods' and next to it is the Tuṣita world, the heaven of delight, the abode of gods who are delighted or satisfied with their condition. Next comes the world of the Nimmānaratidevas, gods who rejoice in their (own) creations, gods who, as the Vimānavatthu commentary (p. 80) assures us, can change their forms at pleasure, or as the Dīgha Nikāya (Vol. III, p. 218) avers, gods who exercise their power over sensual desires created by themselves. The Abhidharmakoṣavyākhyā, the manuscript of which has been examined by Prof. L. de la Vallee Poussin, explains that the Nirmāṇarati gods 'enjoy self-created pleasures, in contrast with the inferior gods who enjoy objects which are presented to them on account of their deserts'.

PART II—HELL

Hells in Buddhist Literature.

Hell (niraya), according to the Buddhist conception, ordinarily seems to be a region situated below the *terrafirma* we tread on. The Visuddhimagga informs us that niraya is so called because it is devoid of the happiness which is the cause of the attainment of sagga and mokkha. It is also called apāya,duggati and vinipāta. Apāya includes tiracchāna (animal kingdom), pettivisaya (peta world), asura world and all hells (II. 427). The universe, according to the Buddhists, consists of many spheres, cakravālas, each of which has its own earth, sun, moon, heavens and hells. (Kern, Indian Buddhism, p. 57).

Hell-one of the six kinds of existence.

Hell is regarded as one of the six kinds of existence, which form the ten dhātus, which, according to some of the schools, possess ten characteristics, namely, (1) form, (2) essential nature, (3) substance, (4) power or force, (5) action, (6) cause, (7) condition, (8) effect, (9) retribution and (10) the final identity.(Yamakami Sogen, Systems of Buddhistic Thought, pp. 275-276).

Hell, a place of punishment for the wrong doer.

Edkins observes from a study of the Chinese works on Buddhism that hell, hungry ghosts and animals are assigned to the wicked. All beings, whether virtuous or vicious, continue to be reborn in one of the six states (e.g. gods, men, monsters, hell, hungry ghosts and animals) until saved by the teaching of the Buddha. (Chinese Buddhism, p. 195).

Position of hell in the universe.

Keith observes in this connection that the universe consists of many world systems, each equipped with earth, heavens and hells, and each system or sphere is divided into three regions (avacaras), worlds (loka) or layers (dhātu), the first, the realm of desire (kāma), the next, of matter or material form (rūpa), and the third that without form (arūpa). In the first are hells or purgatories eight or more in number, while others exist between the spheres (lokantarika); the animal world; the abode of ghosts (pretas); the abode of asuras or demons; which make up the places of punishment (apāya); then comes the abode of men and then six abodes of gods. (Buddhist Philosophy, pp. 92-93).

Mr. Hackmann is right in saying that hell is placed in contrast to heaven. A coarser delineation of reward and punishment in happy or unhappy surroundings replaces the old philosophical conception of existence being a state of suffering, and of the final release from it through the removal of all empirical being. (Buddhism as a Religion, p. 54).

The very lowest of the thirty-one abodes of

The principal hells.

living beings are the hells or places of punishment where the departed spirits have to undergo tortures in consequence of the evil deeds done by them while on earth. The principal hells are eight in number and known by the names of Sañjīva, Kālasūtra, Saṅghāta, Raurava, Mahāraurava, Tapana, Pratāpana and the very deepest, Avīci. Apart from these, there are the Lokāntarika hell and many minor hells. In the old system of the Northern Buddhists, there are, besides the eight hot hells, as many cold hells : Arbuda, Nirarbuda, Aṭaṭa, Hahava, Huhava, Utpala, Padma and Mahāpadma. The Pāli canon mentions the same number and a few more; Aṭaṭa, Abbuda, Nirabbuda, Ahaha, Ababa, Kumuda, Uppalaka, Sogandhika, Puṇḍarīka and Paduma. In later northern works the number of hells is still greater. (Kern, Indian Buddhism, p. 58). Above the hells is placed the animal kingdom. Higher than the animal kingdom is the abode of pretas, ghosts, spectres, though these beings are also placed in the Lokāntarika hell. The hells, together with the next three worlds, constitute the four Apāyalokas or places of suffering. (Ibid, p. 59).

The Wou-kan.

According to the Chinese account, the lowest hell is the Wou-kan, the hell without interval (avīci) i.e. without interval of rest, a place of incessent torment. It is the lowest of the places of torment. (Beal, A Catena of Buddhist Scriptures, p. 57).

Childers' view.

Childers shows from a consideration of what is stated in the Pāli text that there are eight Mahānarakas or principal hells. Besides these, there is the Lokantarika hell which is a place of punishment. It is partly inhabited by pretas. There are many minor hells. The Buddhist hell is a place of torment in which former sins are expiated, but it is only a temporary state and may be immediately followed by re-birth in one of the higher devalokas. (Pāli Dictionary, p. 260).

Six Charles Eliot-Hells are places of temporary, not eternal, punishment.

Sir Charles Eliot points out that the Buddhist hells are temporary. They cannot be regarded as places of eternal punishment. The denizens of these hells have the power of fighting for the acquisition of merit but the task being difficult, one may repeatedly be born in hell. (Hinduism & Buddhism, Vol. I., p. 338).

A layman's religion.

There are many places of torment, to which those go whose conduct has been bad in act, word, or thought or who have been guilty of some one atrocious crime, such as that of the slanderer of Sāriputta, or that of Devadatta, when he drew blood from the Buddha's foot. Such and such a character or the doer of such and such a deed is frequently said to be "as good as cast already into hell," just as the virtuous are said to be "as good as gone to heaven already." The doctrine of heaven and hell is thus especially the layman's religion. (Copleston, Buddhism, Primitive & Present, p. 140.)

Hell in the Nikāyas.

The Nikāyas, the earliest portion of the Pāli Buddhist literature, contain some interesting information regarding the hells. The Aṅguttara Nikāya assures us that a bhikkhu who has no faith in the Buddha and on the other hand, is shameless, lazy and unwise, goes to hell after death. (Aṅguttara Nikāya, Vol. III, p. 3). The same Nikāya adds that a bhikkhu who is wicked or is an evil doer, who does unholy deeds, who commits sin secretly, who pretends to be a samaṇa, who is not a brahmacārī although he pretends to be one, who is foolish and who is full of impurities, after death goes to hell. If such a bhikkhu accepts charity from Brahmins and Ksatriyas and accepts salutation from them, he after death, goes to hell. (Ibid, Vol. IV., pp. 129-130). Nanda's mother, Veḷukantakī, said to Sāriputta that her husband after death, was reborn as a yakkha and had appeared before her in his former birth. (Ibid, p. 66). A person who is wicked, jealous and miserly, is thrown into hell. He who has no such vices goes to heaven. (Ibid, Vol. I, p. 105).

Those who commit sin by body, mind and

Yama and the hell-guards—their functions.

speech go to hell and there the nirayapālā (hell guards) take them to Yama, the ruler of the infernal regions, and speak to him thus, " These men were not devoted to parents, to Samaṇas and Brāhmaṇas and not respectful to superiors and it is for this reason they deserve punishment." Yama asks the sinners, " Have you not seen my first messenger ?" They answer in the negative. He again asks them, " Have you not seen any old person having shaky teeth, grey hair, wrinkled skin, walking with a trembling body ?" They reply in the affirmative. Yama further asks, " Seeing such a person and knowing that you are subject to death, did not any such thought arise in your mind that you should commit meritorious deeds in body, mind and speech ?" They reply, " On account of indolence no such thought arose in our mind." Yama says, " As you have committed sins and not obeyed your parents nor your senior kinsmen, friends, nor any Samaṇa or Brāhmaṇa, nor brother or sister, you are to suffer the consequence of your own demerit." Then they are taken away from Yama. He asks another set of sinners, " Have you not seen my second messenger ?" They reply in the negative. Yama again asks, " Have you not seen any diseased man or woman wallowing in his (or her) own urine and stool ?" They reply, " Yes." Yama asks them the same questions as before and says they are to suffer on account of the sins committed by themselves and not by their parents, friends, relatives, etc. Yama then asks another set of sinners, " Have you not seen a man or woman lying dead for a day or two or three, swollen, turned blue and having pus in the dead body ?" They reply in the affirmative and they are subjected to the same set of questions and answers as before.

Five kinds of punishment

The hell-guards inflict five kinds of punishment :—(1) They strike hot iron nails into the hands and feet in the centre of the chest of the sinners who are to suffer in hell as long as the sins are not exhausted ; (2) They cut the sinners with an axe ; (3) They cut and polish the skin of the sinners with an axe ; (4) They thrust them into a red-hot iron jar with their feet upwards and heads hanging downwards. They then put the red-hot iron jar on a mountain of burning charcoal. They are boiled in the jar as it is rolled upwards and downwards ; (5) They are yoked to a chariot and repeatedly driven backward and forward along a path which is as hot as fire and which gives out flames (Aṅguttara Nikāya, Vol. I, pp. 138-141). It is distinctly stated in the Commentary on the Aṅguttara Nikāya that the Avīci hell is called the mahāniraya (Manorathapūraṇī, p. 408), which has four corners and four gates.

The Avīci Hell.

It is divided into equal compartments and surrounded on all sides by an iron wall. Its lid is made of iron. It has an iron floor which is blazing and giving out flames. Its area is a hundred yojanas. (Aṅguttara Nikāya, Vol. I, pp. 141-142). According to Buddhaghosa, a sinner is made to lie down on his back and his body becomes three leagues (long) in hell. Iron spears are then passed through his right hand palm, his left hand palm, right and left legs and the chest. He is struck with a big axe, profuse blood flows from the wounds which are moreover burnt by fire issuing out of the iron floor. The sinner is cut into six or eight pieces. (Manorathapūraṇī, Sinhalese edition, p.207). The nirayapālās referred to above are officers of hell who carry out the orders of Yama. (Manorathapūraṇī, p. 405)

Punishment according to the Saṁyutta Nikāya.

According to the Saṁyutta Nikāya the Buddha is credited with the opinion that a person will suffer the consequence of whatever may preponderate as between an act and the forbearance from it, that is to say, if the period during which a man abstains from cruelty and homicide is of a longer duration than the period during which he kills animals, he will not go to hell. (Saṁyutta Nikāya, Vol. IV., p. 317 foll).

Hell in the Jātakas.

The Jātakas also furnish us with some information about hell and the deeds that lead to it. In Buddha's time those who took refuge in the three gems had not to go to hell. (Jātaka, Fausboll Vol. I,

p. 96). A king named Kalābu tried to kill the Bodhisatta who was then a rishi and in consequence of this sin, he fell into the Avīci hell. (Ibid, Vol. III, p. 42). Devadatta who spoke falsehood, was swallowed up by the earth and at last fell into the Avīci hell. (Ibid, Vol. III, p. 454, see also Vol. IV, p. 158). King Cetiya had to suffer in the Avīci hell because he indulged in falsehood and abused a rishi. (Ibid, Vol. III, p. 460). A person named Adhamma fell into the Avīci hell for having opposed the Bodhisatta who, at the time, bore the name of Dhamma. (Ibid, Vol. IV, p.103). An acelaka promised not to divulge any secret but he fell into the Avīci hell in consequence of having broken this promise (Ibid, Vol. V, p. 87).The Jātakas speak of two hells, Khuradhāra and Koṭisimbali. In the *Khuradhāra hell*, the hellish creatures are dragged along a floor strewn with razors having very sharp edges. Those who cause *miscarriage* have to suffer in this hell. (Ibid, Vol. V. 274). In the *Koṭisimbaliniraya*, there is a Simbali tree on the bank of the river Vaitaraṇī with blazing branches and leaves hanging over the water. Among the hellish creatures suffering in the river, those who are guilty of adultery, attempt to get out of the river by those branches and as soon as they get up with the help of the blazing branches, they are burnt. (Ibid, Vol. V, pp. 275-276).

Two Hells.

King Nimi was taken by Mātali, the charioteer of Indra, to visit the hells. At first he went to the Vaitaraṇī river where the guards of hell were beating the hellish creatures with burning swords, spears, clubs, etc., and the hellish creatures unable to bear the torture, used to drop down into the river Vaitaraṇī covered with canes full of thorns. The hellish creatures suffered much, being cut into pieces by thorns and from the bottom of the river came out burning spears as long as palm trees. Pierced by these spears, they suffered intolerable tortures. Those who being stout and strong, oppress those who are poor and physically weak, have to suffer in the Vaitaraṇī river. Nimi saw in one place hell-dogs devouring the hellish creatures who in their previous births were misers, abusers of the samaṇas and brāhmaṇas, jealous and mischievous. Thence the King Nimi went to another place in hell where he saw hellish creatures being dragged over a burning floor, for having been in their former existence envious of men and women. At another place he saw a heap of burning charcoal in which were being thrown those hellish creatures who in their former existence, improperly took possession of the wealth accumulated by others for the performance of meritorious deeds. He also saw hellish creatures suffering in a big iron jar which was burning terribly, these creatures in their former existence, harboured

Nimi's visit to hell.

envy against pious samaṇas and brāhmaṇas. He further saw hellish creatures cutting their own necks and throwing them into hot water. He saw others trying to quench their thirst by drinking water from a river but it dried up the moment they attempted to take a sip. The hellish creatures shrieked as they were beaten. He saw in another part of the hell a big lake full of urine and excreta and the creatures oppressed by hunger were devouring these things. Another lake was full of blood and pus and the people parching with thirst were seen drinking them. Some hellish creatures were seen being dragged by means of hooks attached to their tongue. They were horrible to look at. (Nimi Jātaka, (Fausboll) Vol. VI, p. 104, foll).

The fire of hell.

The Buddhists hold that the Fire of Hell is far hotter than any ordinary fire. A tiny stone cast into any ordinary fire, will smoke for a whole day without rumbling. But a rock as big as a pagoda, cast into the Fire of Hell, will crumble in an instant.

No total destruction of the inhabitants of hell.

As for the living beings that are reborn in Hell, no matter how many thousand years they are tormented therein, they go not to destruction. (Buddhist Parables, p. 215). It is because of the power of Kamma that the inhabitants of hell, no matter how many thousands of years they are tormented in hell, are not totally destroyed. Right there are they born, right there do they die. Moreover the Exalted One said, " He shall not die so long as the Evil Kamma is is not exhausted." (Ibid, p. 216). Those living beings who are truly guilty of evil deeds, guilty of evil words, guilty of evil thoughts, defamers of the Noble, holders of wrong views—followers of courses of conduct corresponding to wrong views—these living beings upon dissolution of the body, are reborn in hell. (Dīgha N., Vol. I., p. 82.) Those monks and brāhmaṇas who hold the doctrine that there is no harm in the pleasures of the senses, consort with nuns and fall into the slough of the pleasures of the sen es, on the dissolution of the body, are reborn in hell where they experience sharp bitter se.sations of pain on account of the pleasures of the senses. (Majjhima Nikāya, Vol. I., p. 307.) A man who is a murderer, a thief, an adulterer, a liar, a backbiter, a holder of false views, upon dissolution of body, is reborn in hell. (Buddhist Parables, p. 280). If any person violates the precepts, he or she is smitten with the punishments of hell. (Ibid, p. 309). Those persons who induce sensual, misanthropic, or mentally confused states in others and cause them to lose earnestness, will after death be reborn in purgatory. (Psalms of the Brethr.n, p. 369). If any of the Buddha's disciples does not obey the rules of conduct, five losses are incurred by him. By neglect he incurs great loss of property, a bad report of him goes about, if he goes into any company whether of warriors or of brāhmaṇas or of householders or of ascetics, he enters it without confidence and in confusion; at the moment of death he is bewildered and after death and the dissolution of the body, he goes to some evil condition or place of torment or hell. (Copleston, Buddhism, p. 139). Anyone who slanders or ridicules an ariya, a disciple of the Buddha or pa cekabuddha will be transferred to the Avīci naraka till the end of a kalpa. (Visuddhimagga, Vol. II., p. 425). He will then be born as a wandering hungry ghost and after a thousand kalpas he becomes an animal. After a thousand kalpas more he will again become a man.

The opinion the Buddhists hold on the forgiveness of sin is, that it can be obtained by repentance and meritorious deeds. A definite amount of gifts and worship will bring about the removal of a corresponding amount of sin and its attendant sufferings. Thus a filial daughter, by a certain number of days spent in worshipping a Bodhisatta or a Buddha, can obtain the rescue of a mother from hell (Edkins, Chinese Buddhism, p. 196.)

Situation of the hells, Avīci and Yāmanarakas.

The Buddhist hells, the prisons of the lost, are in some cases situated underneath the region inhabited by man. Twenty thousand yojanas (280,000 miles) below the Jambu continent is one called the Avīci hell or the "Hell of unintermitted torments." The Yāma naraka is half-way between. (Ibid, p. 225). In the Petavatthu there is a reference to the Sattussada hell which is a horrible spectacle. Ambasakkhara, a Licchavi, who was the doer of an evil deed, was reborn in it. It is a hideous place of torment (p. 46). Here a sinner is tied with five kinds of fetters, hot iron is placed upon him, he is laid on a mountain of burning charcoal, then he is thrown into a hot iron jar and he is made to enter a forest where the leaves of the trees are pointed and sharp-edged like swords, afterwards he is made to cross the river Baitaraṇī and lastly he is thrown into the great hell. It is called Sattussada because seven kinds of horrible tortures are inflicted one after the other in this hell. (Petavatthu commentary, p. 221). There is a reference to another hell called the Padumaniraya. It is difficult to ascertain exactly the lease of life of sinners in this hell. The length of life in the Abbuda hell is equal to the time taken in exhausting sesamum seeds measuring twenty *khārikas* by throwing away the grains one after another for a hundred years. The length of life of a sinner in the Nirabbuda hell is more than twenty times the life of a sinner in the Abbuda hell and likewise the period of existence goes up in each of the following—Ababa, Aṭaṭa, Ahaha, Kumuda. Sogandika, Uppala, Puṇḍarīka

Horrors of hells.

The length of a sinner's life in hell.

and the Paduma. (Saṁyutta Nikāya, Vol. I, p. 152). It was in the Padumaniraya, the very last in this series, that a bhikkhu named Kokālika who rebuked Sāriputta and Moggallāna and hated them, had to suffer for an immeasurably long period. This information was given to the Buddha by Brahmā Sahaṁpati. (Saṁyutta Nikāya, Vol I, p. 151. cf. the Dhammapada-aṭṭhakathā, Vol. IV, pp. 91-93). There is a reference to the Lohakumbhiniraya. Four seṭṭhiputtas (banker's sons) used to spend their money and time by indulging in various vices, e.g. adultery, kidnapping and so on and as a consequence they had to suffer in the Lohakumbhi hell. (Dhammapada commentary, Vol. II, pp. 10-11). There is a reference to the Mahāniraya where Devadatta had to suffer being devoured by the earth. We know that he bore bitter malice against the Buddha, tried to take his life, brought about disunion in the Saṁgha and did many other evil and sinful deeds. In consequence of all these terrible sins, he fell into the Mahāniraya. (Sumaṅgalavilāsinī, pt. I, pp. 138-139; cf. Itivuttaka, p. 85.).

Hells in the Sutta Nipāta.

The Sutta Nipāta of the Khuddaka Nikāya of the Sutta Piṭaka speaks of twenty Abbuda hells, twenty Nirabbuda hells, twenty Ababa hells, twenty Ahaha hells, twenty Aṭaṭa hells, twenty Kumuda hells, twenty Sogandhika hells, twenty Uppalaka hells and twenty Pundarīka hells. (S.B.E., Vol. X., p. 121).

Speaking of the Brahmins born in the family of the followers of the hymns (of the Vedas), the Sutta Nipāta says that they are continually caught in sinful deeds, and are to be blamed in this world while in the coming world hell awaits them. Birth does not save them from hell. (Sutta Nipāta, P.T.S., p. 24). A foul-mouthed, false, ignoble, blasting, wicked, evil-doing, low, sinful and base born man should not be garrulous otherwise he would become an inhabitant of hell. (Sutta Nipāta, P.T.S., 128). In hell one is struck with iron hooks, to the iron stake with sharp edges he goes, then he has to swallow as food a red-hot ball of iron. He is made to lie on a bed of embers and has to enter a blazing pyre. He is then boiled in a huge iron pot. He who commits sin is sure to be boiled in a mixture of matter and blood, in water full of worms. (Sutta Nipāta, P.T.S., pp. 129-130). In hell there is the origination of suffering but there is no indication of the path leading to the cessation of it. (Yamaka, P.T.S., Vol. I, p. 179).

Among the denizens of the infernal regions we should perhaps include the Kālakañjaka asuras. In the Kathāvatthu we read that the Kālakañjaka asuras are like petas in their complexion and also in their food, wealth and longevity and the Vepacittiparisādevas are like petas in colour, food, wealth and longevity. (Kathāvatthu, Vol. II., p. 360).

Stories in the Dhammapada Commentary regarding sinners who went to hell.

The Dhammapada commentary narrates many stories furnishing much information regarding hell. There was a peasant at Benares who used to cultivate his fields with the help of a bull which was very lazy. He tried several times to correct its indolence but in vain. At last he grew so very angry with it that he covered the bull with hay and set fire to it with the result that the bull was burnt to death. As a result of this evil deed, he had to suffer for a long time in hell and to work out the last remnants of the sin accruing from his misdeed, he was reborn seven times as a crow which lost its life in fire. (Dhammapada commentary, III, 40-41).

A woman exasperated with her dog, tied a jar full of sand to its neck, threw it into water and thus killed it. In consequence of this evil deed, she had to suffer in hell for a long time. At last for hundred births she was thrown into water with a jar full of sand tied to her neck. (Dhammapada commentary, Vol. III., pp. 41-42).

A jeweller was one day engaged in cooking meat when he received from King Pasenadi a diamond with an order to bore a hole in its centre and send it back at once. The jeweller was in the habit of offering alms daily to a bhikkhu who was present there at that time. He placed the diamond in sight of the bhikkhu and went to wash his hands. After coming back to the spot, he could not find the diamond which during his absence had been swallowed up by his tame crane, which had mistaken it for a lump of flesh. The jeweller however suspected the bhikkhu. Though his wife urged that the bhikkhu was quite innocent, he was not convinced and gave the bhikkhu such a good beating that his head broke and blood came out of it. The tame crane came to suck the blood and the jeweller angrily kicked it with the result that it died instantaneously. The bhikkhu told him to cut the dead crane up, assuring him that the diamond would be found inside its stomach. The crane was cut up and on examining its entrails the diamond was found. As a result of this misdeed, the jeweller after death was reborn in hell. (Ibid, Vol. III., pp. 34-37). Mahāmoggallāna born as a kulaputta of Benares in a previous birth, was induced by his wife to murder his parents. In consequence of this sin, he had to suffer in hell for many years. (Ibid, Vol. III, pp. 68-69). A king of Benares appointed a person to guard one of his frontier provinces against thieves who made frequent incursions there. It was his duty to look to the safety of travellers crossing the disturbed frontier. Once a traveller with his beautiful wife arrived and sought his aid. The guard told them that he would help them to cross the border next morning. In the meantime, being enamoured of the beauty of the traveller's wife, he tried to win her. The evil-minded guard concealed a gem inside the cart of the traveller, announced its loss and kicked up a row over it. To find out the gem, he had the traveller's cart searched, and naturally, the gem was discovered there. He killed the traveller on a charge of theft. For this sin he had to suffer in the Avīci hell. (Dhammapada commentary, Vol. III., pp. 150-151).

Ciñcā, a female devotee of the Nigaṇṭhas, brought a false charge of adultery against the Samaṇa Gotama. In consequence of this evil deed, she was devoured by the earth in the presence of the Buddha and then she fell into the Avīci hell. (Dhammapada commentary, Vol. III., pp. 178-181).

A cowkiller used to slaughter cows daily and sell them. Without beef he could not eat rice. Once it so happened that having left a piece of flesh with his wife, he went to bathe but an intimate friend of her came in the meantime and took it away. The cowkiller on hearing this at once set out, cut the tongue of a cow and ate it after having it duly cooked. On account of this sin he had to suffer in the Avīci hell. (Dhammapada commentary, Vol. III., pp. 332-334).

A banker named Tagara in a previous birth killed his brother's only son for money. Hence he was reborn seven times without any son and his property was confiscated seven times by the king. He had to suffer in hell for many years on account of this sin. At the time of King

Pasenadi of Kosala, he was reborn as a seṭṭhi who was sonless and having died without any issue, his property was confiscated by the king. All his previous merits had been exhausted and as no new merit was accumulated he had to suffer in the Mahāroruva hell. (Dhammapada commentary ,Vol. IV., pp. 77-79).

Hell in the Itivuttaka.

The Itivuttaka records that it is the word of the Buddha that those who commit sins in body, mind and speech are reborn in hell after death. (Itivuttaka, p. 99, Ibid., p. 12). Those who become conceited on account of wealth and fame are reborn in hell after death. (Ibid, p. 73).

Hell in the Visuddhimagga.

The Visuddhimagga also tells us how the commission of sins during life leads to sufferings in hell, and it gives a description of some of the hells. Avīci Hell measures ten thousand yojanas. (Visuddhimagga, Vol. I., p. 207). Buddha by his supernatural power showed the Avīci hell by dividing the earth into two parts at Sāketa. (Visuddhimagga, Vol. II., p. 390). Kāmadhātu exists in the sphere below which is the Avīci Hell and above it the Paranimmitavasavattīdevaloka. (Visuddhimagga, Vol. II., p. 486).

Hells in the Pañcagatidīpanaṁ.

Interesting information with regard to the different hells is also given by the Pañcagatidīpanaṁ. Sañjīva, Kālasutta, Saṅghāta, Roruva, Mahāroruva, Tapa,

Mahātapa and Avīci are the eight mahānirayas. Those who kill and cause living beings to be killed out of lobha, moha, bhaya and kodha, must go to the Sañjīva hell. They suffer in this hell for one thousand years, being tormented again and again without losing life and consciousness. Those who cause injury or do harmful deeds to friends and parents, speak falsehood and backbite others, have to go to the Kālasutta hell. In this hell they are cut to pieces with burning saws just as timber is cut into planks by carpenters, after being marked off with their measuring thread. Those who kill goats, sheep, jackals, hares, deer, pigs, etc., are consigned to the Saṅghāta hell where they are huddled up in one place and then beaten to death. Those who cause mental and bodily pain to others, or cheat others or again are misers, have to proceed to the Roruva hell where they make terrible noise while being burnt in the terrific fire of this hell. Those who steal things belonging to gods, Brahmins and preceptors, those who misappropriate the property of others kept in trust with them and those who destroy the things entrusted to their care, are cast into the Mahāroruva hell where they make a more terrible noise while being consumed by a fire, fiercer than that in the Roruva. Those who cause the death of living beings by throwing them into dāvadaha fire, etc., have to go to Tapa hell where they have to suffer being burnt in a dreadful fire. Those who cause the death of beings by throwing them into greater dāvadaha fire, etc., must go to Mahātapa hell where they have to suffer still more by being burnt in a greater fire. Those who are nihilists and who represent dhamma to be adhamma and *vice versa* must go to Patāpana hell where they suffer by being burnt in fires tnat are more terrific still. Those who injure men of greater virtue and those who kill arahats, parents or preceptors must sink into the Avīci hell where they suffer, being burnt in such a terrific fire that would consume even the hardest things. In this hell there is not the least wave of happiness ; it is therefore called the Avīci or waveless. (Pancagatidīpanaṁ, J.P.T.S., 1884, pp. 154-155).

Ussadaniraya.

Each hell has four Ussadanirayas namely, Miḷhakūpa, Kukkula, Asipattavana and Nadī. Those who are in the mahāniraya, have to proceed to Miḷhakūpa when released. In this terrible hell, they are bitten by a host of worms. Thence they go to Kukkula where they are fried like mustard seeds on a burning pan. Coming out of Kukkula they find before them a beautiful tree full of fruits and flowers where they take shelter for relief from the torments. As soon as they reach the tree, they are attacked by birds of prey such as vultures, owls, etc., having bills as hard as iron and also by carnivorous beasts, dogs, etc. They are killed by these animals which make a repast on their flesh. Those who fight in battle and kill each other will when in hell, be endowed with nails as brilliant as burning swords of iron with which they will scratch each other's body. Those who commit adultery will, in hell, be forcibly compelled to embrace horrible female figures of red-hot iron that will clasp them round and eat up their flesh. Those who are traitors will go to Asipattavana where they are torn and eaten up by bitches, vultures, owls, etc. Those who steal money will also suffer in Asipattavana hell by being compelled to swallow iron balls and molten brass. Those who kill cows and oxen, suffer in hell by being eaten up by dogs having large teeth. Those who kill aquatic animals, e.g. fish, will have to go to the fearful Vaitaraṇī river where the water is as hot as molten brass, and there they will suffer for long ages. Those who prostitute justice by accepting bribes, will be cut to pieces in an iron wheel. (Ibid, pp. 155-156). Those who cause physical pain to others by various means are beaten with clubs and pressed under machines and mountains. Those who create quarrel between friends are led along a path as sharp as the edge of a razor. Those who destroy paddy have to suffer in the Kukkula hell.

Those who earn their livelihood by dishonest means are eaten up by worms in pits full of impurities. Those who are envious, cherish anger, or become happy at the sight of the sufferings of others, are reborn after death in Yamaloka and the demon world. (Pañcagatidīpanaṁ, p. 156). Those who cherish great anger in their hearts are reborn as swans and pigeons, etc. Those who are fools are reborn as insects. Those who are haughty and angry are reborn as snakes. Those who neglect their friends on account of pride are reborn as asses and dogs. Those who are jealous and miserly are reborn as monkeys. Those who are garrulous, fickle and shameless are reborn as crows. Those who give trouble to elephants and horses, etc., are reborn as parrots and scorpions, etc. Those who are miserly, irritable and fond of backbiting are reborn as tigers, cats, bears, etc. Those who are charitable but at the same time cherish anger, are reborn as nāgas with great miraculous powers. Those who are charitable but angry and haughty at the same time are reborn as big garuḍas. (Pañcagatidīpanaṁ, pp. 156-157). Those who are deceitful and charitable are reborn as great asuras. (Ibid, p. 158). The Kalakañja asuras are classed as petas.

The Buddhist conception of hell compared with the Brahmanical idea.

A comparison with the Brahmanical idea of hell will show that the conception of the infernal regions is very much the same in the two systems. The names are often the same and the tortures described in the literature of the respective faiths have much in common. We give below some excerpts from the Mārkaṇḍeya Purāṇa to illustrate our observations. Any other Purāṇa would have done equally well, the difference between one Purāṇa and another being but slight.

The fruition of karma —according to the Mārkaṇḍeya Purāṇa.

About the philosophy of the fruition of *Karma* or the good and evil deeds, we read in the Mārkaṇḍeya Purāṇa that a man's merit or demerit depends on good or bad deeds done by him. Whatever is good yields pleasant and praiseworthy result, and whatever is evil yields painful and abominable result. A virtuous man or a doer of good deeds is bold and straightforward. Undaunted by anything, he lives, moves and has his being in happiness. But a sinner tells a lie, he is frightened at the slightest sound, his heart throbs, and he cannot withstand the dangers that always stare him in the face. Man's existence on earth requires him to do deeds, good or bad. His action produces a change in his mind. His good deeds are consumed by his living in the company of immortal beings in heaven, by the enjoyment of happy and pleasant results and by sharing joys with Gandharvas, Siddhas and Apsarasas. Man's evil deeds are also consumed by his undergoing various torments day and night within hell. Thus a man's good deeds springing as they do from virtue, are accompanied by pleasures; while his evil deeds engendered by sin are characterised by pain. (Pargiter, Mārkaṇḍeya Purāṇa, pp. 77-78).

Hells in the Mārkaṇḍeya Purāṇa.

The various hells are thus described in the same Purāṇa. Raurava is in truth two thousand yojanas in size. There is a cavity containing burning charcoal into which sinners are thrown. Their feet are burnt day and night, and they run about for over a thousand yojanas until they are released from this hell and cast into a similar one. (Pargiter, The Mārkaṇḍeya Purāṇa, p. 68). The Mārkaṇḍeya Purāṇa further points out that in the Mahāraurava hell, the earth, to the extent of thirty-five yojanas, is made of copper ; beneath it is fire that keeps the whole region hot. Here the sinner is thrown with his hands and legs tied together. Scorched by the heat, he rolls about. He is attacked by crows, herons, wolves and owls, scorpions, mosquitoes and vultures. Burnt by fire and confounded by beasts, he cries at the top of his voice, " Father ! Mother ! Brother ! Dear one !" Sinners attain emancipation after suffering in this manner.

Tamas is another hell. It is bitterly cold, but enveloped in darkness. Unable to endure cold, sinners here clasp one another in vain to obtain relief. They are plagued by hunger and thirst. Thus they endure great afflictions until their sins are completely consumed.

Then there is another hell named Nikrintana.

Here revolve the potter's wheels. Sinners are cut by the string of Fate and mounted on the wheels, and their severed parts reunite. Thus sinners are cut asunder during thousands of years until the whole of their sins are consumed. Apratishṭa is the name of another hell where sinners whirl around, spit out blood continually and endure pain intolerable to living creatures.

Asi-patra-vana is the name of another hell, the floor of which is ' covered with blazing fire for a thousand yojanas . Sinners are to suffer from the scorching rays of the sun. In the midst of this hell there is a beautiful forest wherein the trees have moist leaves with blades as sharp as swords ; within this forest powerful dogs with long muzzles and large teeth bark. When thirsty sinners come to the forest, violent winds begin blowing, the trees hurl down sword-leaves upon them ; and the dogs tear their limbs. The sinners undergo infernal torments and wail in vain.

Then there is another dreadful hell, Tapta-kumbha by name. Sinners are cast head-long into heated pitchers filled with oil, iron and powder and are then boiled. Terrible vultures pull them out, smash their eye-bones and their skulls and again put them into the pitchers. Then they are stirred up with a spoon and are ' churned up in the whirling pool of copious oil.' (Pargiter, Mārkaṇḍeya Purāṇa, pp. 72-74).

The punishment for lewdly gazing on other's

The particular sins that lead to the tortures are thus detailed.

wives and for covetous looks on the possessions of others, is the continual tearing out of their eyes for a thousand years for each sin.

The punishment of sinners—according to the Mārkaṇḍeya Purāṇa.

For giving instruction and advice in wicked shāstras, for improper repetition of the shāstras and for blasphem-ing the Vedas, the gods, the dwijas and their gurus, the punishment is the tearing out of the tongue.

Base men who incite dissension between the nearest and dearest relations are sawn through.

Those who inflict pain, deprive others of the joys of life and cause suffering to innocent men—are placed between the meal and sand.

The person who eats another's śrāddha is rent in twain by birds.

Those that lacerate the heart of good men by their speech are repeatedly struck by birds. The tongue is cut through by razors of those who are guilty of backbiting, falsehood and duplicity. Conceited persons, behaving ungraciously with their parents and gurus are immersed head foremost in pus and urine. Those who eat while others around them remain unfed, are turned into sūci-mukha birds and are made to feed on carrion and exudations.

Those who on earth force a brahmin to take his meal with a man of other caste are fed on ordure here. Whoever appeases his own hunger while a destitute companion goes without food, has to feed on phlegm. The hands of those that touch brahmins, cattle and the fire with unwashed hands are put into fire. Fire is put into the eyes of those who gaze at the sun, moon and stars while the hands and mouth are unwashed.

For touching with the feet, parents, brothers and sisters, gurus, cattle, fire and daughters-in-law, the legs are bound with red-hot fetters and placed in the midst of charcoal, and the sinners are burnt up to the knees. The eyes are torn out with pincers of those who eat unhallowed milk, khichree, goats' flesh and the food offerings to gods. The punishment for listening to blasphemy against gurus, the gods and dwijas and the Vedas, is the thrusting in of red-hot iron wedges into their eyes.

Those who destroy rest-houses, temples, the houses of brāhmaṇas and break up congregations are continually flayed with sharp instruments. Crows pull out the intestines of those who passed urine in the path of cattle, brahmins and the sun. He who causes the bigamy of his own daughter is cut into portions and swept along a burning stream of corrosives. The person who abandons his dependants during famine or other sorts of distress has to feed on pieces of his own flesh. A man who out of avarice gives up a refugee or discards dependants, is tortured by means of machines. Those that obstruct good deeds are ground-down along with gravels.

Breakers of pledges are bound down and devoured by insects and ravens. For committing adultery and having sexual intercourse by day, sinners are made to suffer from hunger and thirst. Sinners are also pinned with iron thorns on the silk-cotton tree. Adulterers are tortured in the 'mouse.'[1] Being compelled to sit in the public road with a huge rock on the head without food is the punishment inflicted on one who pursues the art of his spiritual preceptor by deposing him For discharging phlegm, urine or ordure in water, a person has to live in the midst of those things.

For neglecting the rules of mutual hospitality the punishment is the devouring of each other's flesh. For discarding the Vedas and the fires sinners are flung down from lofty precipices. Old men marrying virgin widows have to become worms and are fed by ants. For all sorts of intercourse with an outcaste a man is turned into an insect living under stones. For eating without sharing the food with those who look on, a man is made to devour burning charcoal. The backs of backbiters are continually devoured by wolves. Base ungrateful men are made blind, deaf and dumb and have to wander without food.

Evil-minded treacherous persons are dropped into Tapta Kumbha, then ground down, next cast into Kurambhabāluka̅, put through mechanical tortures and rent with serrated leaves, divided by

[1] **A kind of instrument of torture.**

the thread of Fate—yet expiation is long to come.

Corrupt brahmins for violence during śrāddhas have to drink their own perspiration. Gold-stealers, slayers of brahmins, drunkards and defilers of their guru's bed are consumed in hell-fire and then born again as diseased persons. Birth and death thus continue till the end of the kalpa. A cow-slayer goes to hell during three births. Below is a list of the strata of life into which different sinners are born on release from hell.

A dwija is born as an ass for having accepted a valuable gift from an outcaste and as an worm for having sacrificed for such.

For coveting a spiritual preceptor's wife or property, one is reborn as a dog. For scorning parents, as an ass; for abusing them, a grackle; and for scorning a brother's wife, a pigeon; while for injuring her, the punishment is to be born as a tortoise.

A man is born a monkey when he pursues not his brother's welfare while eating his piṇḍa. For embezzlement one is reborn as a worm; the detractor as a Rākshasa and the traitor, a fish. An idiotic person who out of folly carries off crops is born as large mouthed ichneumon-like rat.

For lustfully touching a man's wife—the birth of a wolf. For adultery with brother's wife—a man has to become a dog, a jáckal, a heron, a vulture, a snake and a bird of prey in succession.

For adultery with a guru's wife, friend's wife and the king's wife one becomes a male-cuckoo. The libertine becomes a hog.

For obstructing sacrifices, marriages and liberality—one becomes a worm. For obtaining food without offering it to the gods and pitris—one becomes a crow and for scorning the eldest brother, a curlew. A sūdra approaching a brahmin woman becomes a worm and by begetting children by her, a wood-boring insect. A caṇḍāla for the same offence becomes a hog, a worm and a diver bird.

The murderer of a woman or the child-slayer becomes a worm while for killing an unarmed man—an ass; but by stealing food one becomes a fly. Punishments vary according to the kind of food stolen. For stealing rice-food one is born a cat; the same with sesamun and oil cake—a rat; clarified butter—an ichneumon; for venison—a hawk and so on. For stealing distilled spirits one becomes a francolin partridge. There are similar punishments for stealing different objects, e.g., for stealing iron one is-born a crow, for brass a green pigeon and so on.

For stealing learning, for not rewarding the guru and for making another's wife one's own —a man is born an eunuch after release from hell. For improper "Homa" oblation one becomes a dyspeptic. The after-characteristics of men released from hell are—abusiveness, coarseness, cruelty, treachery, flirting with other men's wives, contempt of the gods, dishonesty, fradulence, avarice and assassination—in fact the performance of whatever is forbidden (Pargiter, Mārkaṇḍeya Purāṇa, pp. 78-88).

The difference between the Buddhist and Brahmanical conceptions, it will be observed, is this that in the Buddhist system respect for the bhikkhus is ordained and gifts to them produce very great merit while in the Brahmanical system, it is reverence for the Ṛṣis and Brāhmaṇas and acts of charity to them that secure the heavenly pleasures, and the opposite conduct in both cases leads to hell. It is interesting to note that sufferings in hell as described in the Buddhist and Jain books are almost identical. A perusal of the foregoing pages gives us a fairly accurate idea of sufferings in Buddhist hells. Among the Jains we know on the authority of the Uttarādhyayanasūtra that in hell there is suffering from heat and cold (Jaina Sūtras, II, 93., S.B.E., Vol. XLV). The same work also tells us that there the sinners are cut, pierced and hacked to pieces with swords and daggers, with darts and javelins (Ibid., p. 94). They undergo sharp, acute and horrible pain. (Ibid., pp. 96-97) The Sūtrakritāṅga, a Jain work of great importance, tells us that the sinners who commit evil deeds and injure many beings without repentance, go

Both Buddhist and Jain ideas of sufferings in hell are almost identical.

to hell, and cross the river Vaitaraṇī the waves of which cut like sharp razors. They are pierced with long pikes and tridents. They roll about and are roasted in the Kadambavālukā river. They come to the great impassable hell called Asūrya (i.e. where the sun does not shine); here they are roasted. There is another hell called the Santakshana. Here the sinners are hewn with axes like pieces of timber. They are stewed in iron cauldrons filled with their own blood. They are not reduced to ashes. They undergo this sort of punishment for their misdeeds. Besides these hells named above, there are other hells where sinners suffer in consequence of their sinful deeds done by them while on earth. The noses, ears and lips of sinners are cut off with razors and their tongues are pulled out with sharp pikes. They are thrown into large cauldrons and boiled there. They are compelled to drink molten lead and copper when they are thirsty. We are further told by the Sūtrakritāṅga that in hell there is a terrible towering mountain called the Vaitālika where evil-doers are tortured for more than a thousand hours. Thus the sinners are tortured day and night. They cry at the top of their voice in a dreadful hell which contains various implements of torture (Jaina Sūtras, Vol. II., pp. 279-285., S.B.E., Vol. XLV).

It is interesting to note that neither in the Buddhist nor in the Brāhmanical system, and in fact, in no Indian religious system, is there any conception of eternal, never-ending suffering in hell, like the Christian, or rather, the Hebrew eschatological conception of *Gehenna*, the abode of the wicked where they suffer endless torments by fire. Some of the Christian fathers no doubt hold that ultimately there would be an end to the punishment of the most wicked as well as of the devils; but this is not the idea of either the early or the mediæval Church, and even Protestant Divines stick to the idea of the never-ending punishment of the damned. This, however, is quite foreign to the Indian conception according to which every act either good or bad, produces happiness or suffering only for a limited period, though the period may be considerably long according to the nature of the deed.

INDEX

Acīravatī, 71
Ajātasattu, 66
Akaniṭṭhakā, 7, 29
Ambasakkhara, 105
Ambavimāna, 88
Anāthapiṇḍika, 23, 36
Andhavana, 62
Anomā, 82
Arūpaloka, 8, 26
Assaka, 74
Atappa gods, 29
Avīci, 98, 104, 111
Avīha gods, 29, 111
Ābhassaraloka, 3, 7, 8
Ānanda, 63

Bandhula, 60
Benares, 49, 50, 56, 108, 109
Bimbisāra, 38, 76
Brahmā, 3
Brahmaloka, 2, 6
Brahmavimāna, 4
Buddhaghosa, 18, 99

Campā, 68
Cātummahārājika, 1, 5, 9, 30, 80
Channa, 82
Chattamānavaka, 39
Ciñcā, 110
Cintāmaṇi, 86
Damila, 22
Devadatta, 95
Dhataraṭṭha, 9, 5
Dinnā, 24
Edkins, 104
Esikā, 65

Gaggarā, 68
Gandhabbas, 9
Gayāgāma, 67
Gopāla, 75
Gopāladevaputta, 89
Guttila, 56, 57

Hackmann, 93
Inda, 10, 13, 22
Isipatana, 49
Itivuttaka, 111

Jambu, 104
Jambudīpa, 32, 33
Jetavana, 52, 55, 80

Kadambavālukā, 125
Kalābu, 100
Kalandanivāpa, 45
Kapilavatthu, 5
Kāmaloka, 8, 26
Kāmāvacaraloka, 2
Kāśī, 73
Keith, 93
Kern, 94
Kevaddha, 1
Khiddāpadosikā, 4
Kiki, 73
Kośala, 41
Krañca, 44
Kumārakassapa, 83
Kuśīnārā, 60
Kuvera, 5

Lohakumbhi hell, 106
Lokāntarika, 94

Magadha, 59
Mahākaccāyana, 74
Mahākassapa, 23, 51
Mahāniraya, 106
Mahāraurava, 111, 112, 117
Mahātapa, 113
Mallikā, 24, 60
Manopadosikā, 4
Manorathapūraṇī, 98
Māyā, 16, 17
Milhakūpa, 113
Moggallāna, 43, 44, 62, 66, 72, 106

Nakkhattakīlaṁ, 46
Namucī, 5
Nandanavana, 39
Nandiya, 25
Nālandā, 53
Nimi, 101
Nimmānarati, 2, 21, 91
Nirabbuda hell, 105

Pajāpati, 10
Paranimmitavasavattī, 2, 21
Pasenadi, 25, 36, 111
Pāṭaliputta, 84
Potana, 74
Poussin, 91
Puṇḍarīka hells, 106

Rakkhāmanta, 9
Rājagaha, 5, 26, 38, 43, 45, 48, 51, 62, 67, 70, 71, 72, 73, 77
Revatī, 69
Roruva, 111
Rūpaloka, 8, 26

Sakka, 1
Santusita, 2, 32
Sattussada, 105
Satyaloka, 3
Sāketa, 111
Sāriputta, 46
Sārnātha, 63, 69
Sāvatthī, 26, 45, 52, 53, 64
Soma, 6, 10
Subhakiṇṇa gods, 29
Sudassī, 7
Sudhamma, 15
Sujāta, 13
Sunetta, 18
Suyāma, 1

Tagara, 110
Taptakumba, 118
Tāvatiṁsa, 30, 63, 71, 72, 73
Tusita, 10, 16

Ujjayinī, 56
Uttaramadhurā, 53

Varuṇa, 10
Vaijayanta, 32
Vaitālika, 125
Vaitaraṇī, 101, 105, 114
Vepacittiparisādeva, 107
Veluvana, 38, 51, 54
Vesālī, 5
Vessāmitta, 5
Visālakkhī, 61
Visuddhimagga, 18, 92, 111

Wou-Kan, 94

Yasuttarā, 63
Yāma, 10, 105

APPENDIX

BOOKS OF STORIES OF HEAVEN AND HELL

Genesis, Chronology and Utility

1. INTRODUCTORY :—The supreme necessity of inculcation of the belief in a life beyond death, in Heaven and Hell, and in distribution of rewards and punishments according to merits and demerits of one's deeds as a means of persuading the people to the path of virtue and of deterring them from the path of vice was realised by some of the Indian teachers long before the advent of the Buddha. This belief was put to the test in the 6th century B.C., when the spirit of sophistry was predominant. This called forth hostile attacks from the materialists, who were divided into two camps—the metaphysical and the politico-moral. The metaphysical school was represented by Ajita Kesakambalī and the politico-moral school came to be associated with the name of Bṛhaspati or Śukra. That which came to be known long afterwards as Cārvāka philosophy was really a synthesis of the teachings of these older schools of thought. The further development of the teaching of Ajita Kesakambalī can be traced in the views of Pāyāsi (Pāesi or Prayāsi), the chieftain of Setavya in Kosala, who came into the field, according to Buddhist evidence, immediately after the demise

of the Buddha, and according to the Jaina evidence, shortly before the Jinahood of Mahāvīra. It is Pāyāsi who discussed the practical issues and supplied the stronger logical arguments of Ajita's philosophy. Among the opponents of Pāyāsi one has to reckon the Venerable Kumāra-samaṇa Kesī, a follower of Pārśva, and the Venerable Kumāra Kassapa, a follower of the Buddha. Among Ajita's many opponents, the chief was Pakudha Kaccāyana. Indian thought, before the advent of Mahāvīra and the Buddha as teachers, was closed with the powerful scepticism or agnosticism of Sañjaya of the Belaṭṭhi clan, who has been expressly identified in the Mahāvastu (III. p. 59) with Sañjaya Parivrājaka of Rājagaha, famous in Buddhist tradition as the previous teacher of Sāriputta and Moggallāna, who became afterwards two chief disciples of the Buddha. Moggallāna and Kumāra Kassapa are two among the immediate disciples of the Buddha who popularised Buddhism amongst the mass by means of drawing in a novel way the pictures of life in Heaven and Hell. It is in their school that there developed a cult which culminated in popular Buddhism as represented by the Birth-stories, the edifying legends, the epic narrations, the songs of praise, including the stories of Heaven and Hell. The greatest pioneer in this missionary movement was Moggallāna who had to pay the tragic penalty of martyrdom to the cause of his religion. He became necessarily an eyesore to Buddha's detractors, the so-called Heretics, on account of the consummate skill with which he is said to have popularised the lofty teachings of his master. In Ajita we meet with an unqualified atheism, in Sañjaya, mere scepticism. Mahāvīra, and still better the Buddha, had shown the way to enlightened belief. The change of teachers on the part of Moggallāna is eloquent of the conflict between enlightened doubt and enlightened faith ending in victory for the latter. Moggallāna was a past master in the art of persuasion by means of miracles of eye-witness to life in Heaven and Hell, and of this art he was by no means the first professor, since he had a long line of precursors before him. In all essentials the art remained the same, only it was accommodated in changed circumstances to time and place. This art is found to have a painful history behind it, with a long list of martyrs, whose accounts are yet to be written. The Buddhist Jātaka Book and the Kauṭiliya Arthaśāstra have recorded only a few typical examples of martyrdom, a host of others being cast into oblivion. A close examination of recorded instances we have, goes to show that there was at the time no other effective way of checking the tyrants and sinners with whom the country abounded than the one resorted to by the Aryan preachers by conjuring up the pictures of life in Heaven and Hell. They succeeded in striking terror in the hearts of wrong-doers, as also they succeeded in inducing the good people into acts of piety by holding up before them the vivid and splendid picture of paradises ready to receive them. In one of the Buddhist Birth-stories[1], the great sage Saṅkicca has narrated the terrible fate that overtook the tyrants and sinners on the dissolution of their mortal frame, after their death. All these he did in reply to an enquiry made by his friend who usurped the throne of Benares after killing his father in secret. The king was terror-stricken, lost the peace of his mind and felt as if he was being tormented in a hell. So he became eager to hear from his friend destinies of transgressors of the moral law after death. The instances cited by the sage are as follows :—

1. Ajjuna, king of the Kekayas, was a great archer. For causing annoyance to the sage Gotama he was utterly destroyed.

2. King Daṇḍakī having insulted Kisavaccha, the guileless ascetic, was uprooted like a palm-tree.

3. King Mejjha fell from his high position for ill-treatment of Mātaṅga, the far-famed sage ; his kingdon became a wilderness : he died with all his subjects.

4. Members of the Andhaka-Veṇhu race were slain by each other's mace in consequence of an insult meted out to Kaṇha-Dīpāyaṇa.

[1] Fausböll, Jātaka, No. 530.

5. Being cursed by a sage, King Cecca capable of flying through the air, was swallowed by the earth.

The Sarabhaṅga-Jātaka[1] adds two more instances of persons suffering torments in Hells :—

6. King Kalābū having maimed the sinless saint, the preacher of patience, was burnt in an infernal abode.

7. King Nāḷikira fell into the jaws of dogs in hell for the inhuman ill-treatment of a guileless ascetic, whose body was torn to pieces and offered to dogs.

The story of Daṇḍakī is expanded in the Sarabhaṅga-Jātaka, that of Mejjha in the Mātaṅga, that of Andhaka-Veṇhu in the Ghata-Jātaka and in the Mausalaparva of the Mahābhārata, that of Kalābū in the Khantivāda-Jātaka and that of Cecca in the Cetiya. In one instance, the tyrannical monarch puts the ascetic to inhuman death by cutting him into pieces and offering his limbs to dogs to devour. In another instance, another king pierces a harmless saint with arrow under the misapprehension that he stood in his way as Ill-Luck to spoil his game. In a third instance, a courtezan, then a brahmin minister, and subsequently the king himself spat on the matted hair of an ascetic as a means of getting rid of sin and putting off calamities. In a fourth instance, the boys roughly handled a great saint

[1] Fausböll, Jātaka, No 522.

as a matter of sport. Circumstances changed by the time of Mahāvīra and the Buddha. It is evident from the reminiscences of these two world-renowned teachers, as recorded in the Jaina Ohāṇa-Sutta[1] and the Buddhist Mahāsīhanāda-Sutta,[2] that within the Aryandom, the central region in Northern India, the mischief-makers were confined to young cowherds. In non-Aryan regions the whole population was against the preachers and missionaries of Aryanism. As we read in the Jaina Āyāraṃga-Sutta, in Lāḍha or Western Bengal, the wild inhabitants used to set dogs upon the ascetics. Some of the Buddhist Suttas, e.g., the Āḷavaka, record chances of ascetics being thrown down precipices, being suspended from trees with head downwards or thrust into holes of monstrous serpents by the savage tribes. These tribes were actuated to this line of conduct, in cases, by a motive of self-defence, as a protection against the mischiefs of the spies disguised as ascetics. To cope with this formidable opposition, the ascetics with their mission of peace found it necessary to fall back upon the only weapon in their hands likely to prove effective, namely, inculcation of moral precepts against vice and in favour of virtue, accompanied by artistic illustrations and religious demonstrations, and in certain cases, by miracles and other supernormal feats. Grim stories of sinners sent to the bottom-

[1] See the Âyāraṃga-Sutta

[2] See the Majjhima-Nikāya.

less pit of hells and of virtuous persons enjoying the bliss of paradises told with effect upon the populace. Painting had its full share in the task. By means of pictures illustrating the terrible doom of sinners and the happy lot of the pious souls, some of the ascetics sought to make a powerful appeal. As Buddhaghosa tells us, a class of beggarly brahmins sprang into being with this as their exclusive profession, and they were known as Nakhas or Maṅkhas. According to Jaina accounts, the parents of Gośāla, the great Ājīvika leader, belonged to this class of ascetics. The Sanskrit drama Mudrārākṣasa draws a picture of the Mauryan time when some of the naked ascetics moved about in the country with Yama-paṭas or Death-pictures in their hands.

These pictures are described in Buddhist literature as Karaṇacitra or Caraṇacitra, praised by the Buddha himself as the very best of the pictorial art of his time. Bas-reliefs and frescoes took the place of these pictures in Buddhism. So long as Buddhism was confined during its earlier history to a region where Aryanism was the accepted creed, the Buddhist preachers did not feel the necessity of laying emphasis on sufferings in hells. But when Buddhism was propagated outside this region among peoples who were not cultured enough to be tolerant and thoughtful, they found it expedient to utilise or invent the ghastly stories of hell, full of pain and sorrow. The Suttanta-

Jātakas representing the earliest forms of Buddhist Birth-stories, tell us only of a glorious life in celestial mansions. The inscriptions of Aśoka are conspicuous by the absence of any reference to hell in them. Among the large number of sculptures carved on the railing of the Barhut Stūpa, we come across only one scene of hell where a man and a woman are suffering torments for the uncondoned sin of poisoning innocent people.[1] Among the many schools of Buddhist thought, particularly among those which are pre-Aśokan, there is only one, viz., the Gokulikas or Kaukkulikas, given to pessimistic speculations, emphasizing the darker aspects of life.[2] Very naturally the Book of Stories of Hell developed within Buddhism later than the Book of Stories of Heaven, as being shown in the following pages.

2. Canonical Background :—Two Canonical anthologies called Peta and Vimānavatthus, the Books of Stories of Heaven and Hell, seem to be, on the whole, two poetical offshoots of the Canonical Jātaka Book. These anthologies inculcating the Buddhist belief in Heaven and Hell, particularly the Book of Stories of Heaven, must be said to have, in some form or other, an important bearing on the Inscriptions of Aśoka. For instance, the expression *vimāna-dasana*[3] is connected with

[1] Cunningham, Stūpa of Bharhut, Pl. XL.2-5.

[2] Preface to the Points of Controversy, (P.T.S.).

[3] Rock Edict IV "*Vimānadasanā ca hastidasanā ca agikhaṃdhāni ca añāni ca divyāni rūpāni dasayitpā*" (Girnar).

the popular religious festivals, all Indian in origin, which were adopted by the Buddhists. The superstitious practice of *Vimāna-dassana* condemned in one of the poems of the Aṭṭhaka group[1] as a folly, found favour with the Buddhists of Aśokan age, and when we search for such practices in the Canon, we find that they are in the Book of Stories of Heaven (Vimānavatthu), where they are canonized on an extensive scale. The conflict between these two feelings naturally indicates a long interval of religious development separating the Vimāna-vatthu from the Book of Octaves in the Sutta-Nipāta. Our presumption is intensified by the Canonical records in hand, which mark the progressive course of the belief in celestial mansions (vimānas). The old Indian current notion of the appearance of a god or an angel in celestial mansions glided as a belief into the Buddhist faith, and the earliest literary expression which this belief assumed is the Legend of Serissakavimāna in the Pāyāsi-Suttanta. In order to ascertain the probable date of the legend, it is essential that we must be aware of the relative position of the Legend and the main Dialogue of which the Suttanta is composed.

3. PĀYĀSI-SUTTANTA :—The Dialogue is a philosophical controversy between Kumāra Kassapa

[1] Sutta-Nipāta IV No. 12, stanza 10 :—
"*Diṭṭhe sute sīlavate mute va ete ca nissāya vimānadassī, vinicchaye ṭhatvā pahassamano 'bālo paro akusalo' ti câha.*"

and Pāyāsi on the future existence of man, which, according to tradition, took place shortly after the death of Gotama. The Venerable Kumāra Kassapa enjoyed, even during Buddha's life-time, the reputation of a "Flower Talker" (Citrakathī), and Pāyāsi, his disputant, was the chieftain of Setavya, who is said to have ruled with an iron hand and wielded an immense influence, and who was an unbeliever and a most cynical atheist. The interest of the controversy lies in this, that a professed atheist and unbeliever like Pāyāsi was at last thrown, by a bitter irony of fate, into a position where he had to appear as an ardent believer. Here ends the controversy as it occurs in the Pāyāsi Discourse, and what follows is a mythical supplement embodying a Vimāna-story, the Serissaka-vimāna,[1] in which the transformed chieftain is made to appear as a god reassuring mankind, through the Venerable Gavampati, who happened to meet the god in his empty or lonely mansion, of a life hereafter and of heavenly glory as a reward for pious gifts here below. The god Pāyāsi is represented as heightening the effect of his message to mankind by a sad contrast between the heavenly rewards which he and his disciple Uttara obtained by dispensing charity with or without the humbleness of spirit.[2] Can there be,

[1] The reading adopted in the P.T.S. edition of the Dīgha is *Sirisaka*.

[2] The chieftain Pāyāsi is said to have been reborn in the lonely *Serissaka* mansion of the lowest heaven in Buddhist cosmography

we ask, a greater irony than this? The powerful chieftain, a veritable atheist, far famed throughout Northern India for his strong materialistic proclivities, to whom all the similies, legends and parables of the 'Flower-Talker' Kassapa, perfectly innocent of all philosophical reasonings, were through almost the whole of the controversy,[1] unavailing as proofs of existence hereafter, of reward and punishment in heaven and hell, and above all, of possibility, the physical possibility, of return from the other world, whether heaven or hell, is not only represented, at the abrupt end[2] of the controversy, as a sincere believer, but what is more, is made to die a believer and appear a god conversing with a Buddhist Thera in his lonely mansion, as if to prove to the world by his present condition how utterly unfounded and baneful was his previous disbelief. The irony of fate does not end here. The Serissaka legend which is strictly speaking a dialogue between Gavampati and Pāyāsi would have us perceive the difference between Pāyāsi and his disciple Uttara in their present conditions, proving the relative worth of gifts, to the priesthood, bestowed

as lesser reward of liberality without humility, while his disciple Uttara got admission to a higher heaven, the Heaven of the Thirty-Three as greater reward of gifts in faith made to Buddhist priests.

[1] Dīgha II. pp 319-349.

[2] Ibid. p. 352, where the chieftain suddenly changes his views as a consequence of a parable of Kassapa, by no means more extraordinary than others which he had been hearing over and over again but which proved futile.

with or without the faith, which is the sole determining factor of values of gifts, irrespective of the question whcther the bestower is himself the owner or an agent through whom the gifts are made.

The reason is not far to seek. The account of the controversy, if scrutinised, leaves a permanent impression that an able controversialist like the chieftain Pāyāsi could not have been convinced by mere similies, parables and legends used as arguments and persuasions, a procedure so common amongst the popular preachers of religion. The account of the controversy fills thirty-six pages in the Pâli Text Society edition of the discourse, and up to the 34th page the strong-minded chieftain avowed that he was not convinced while on the 36th page, he all on a sudden confesses to his conviction. This would seem to any impartial judge most unnatural, as there is nothing exceptionally striking and forcible in the parable between pages 34 and 36, that could persuade and convert the inexorable Pāyāsi, or to induce the critic to believe that the matter had, in fact, ended so triumphantly for the Flower-Talker.

4. Three Dialogues :—The Pāyāsi-Suttanta, as it is, weaves three distinct dialogues within the narrative frame of the Legend of Serissaka Mansion. These three dialogues forming three integral parts of the Suttanta in its present form are so interwoven as to indicate three well-defined stages in the

growth of the Serissaka Legend and so arranged that the second part including the first or the third part including the first and the second presents a complete narrative of its own. The first part which is a dialogue between Pāyāsi and Kumāra Kassapa gives an account of the philosophical controversy, consummated by the latter's religious discourse following the former's conversion. The second part which is a sequel to the first is similarly a dialogue between Pāyāsi and his disciple Uttara, in which the latter succeeds in persuading the former to set up gifts in faith. The dialogue is brought to a close by a brief reference to the heavens where the teacher and the pupil were reborn after death. The third part which is a sequel to the second is also a dialogue between the Venerable Gavampati and the god Pāyāsi, the scene of which is lain in the lonely Serissaka Mansion. The gist of their conversation has already been referred to. It is clear, then, that the three dialogues point to three periods of Pāyāsi's life on earth and in heaven. The first, for instance, is connected with the time when the controversy took place ; the second with an intermediate period which dates from the controversy and extends up to his death and also to the death of his disciple Uttara ; and the third with a time when the chieftain, now a god, had to repent, long after his death and long after the death of Kassapa, over his present condition inferior, if compared with that of his disciple.

Granting that the Pāyāsi-Suttanta, as we now have it, is a connected narrative of the prose legend of Serissaka Mansion, the occurrence of three dialogues can be best accounted for historically only by a theory of theological fabrication passing through two stages. Remembering that Kumāra Kassapa failed by all his flower-talking to convince the strong-minded chieftain, of the future existence of man, a theological fabrication about Pāyāsi's conversion and pious gifts leading to his rebirth as a god in the Serissaka Mansion, would seem possible only when, after the death of Pāyāsi and after the death of Kassapa, people would have but faint memory of the controversy ending in signal defeat for a popular theologian and flower-talker. Conceivably the legend had, at first, no reference exactly to the Serissaka Mansion, such particularisation being possible at a still later date. The earlier tradition probably was that the chieftain Pāyāsi was reborn after his death in the heaven of four guardian angels, while his disciple Uttara achieved greater reward as he was reborn among the gods of the Thirty-three. The legend in this earlier stage afforded a nucleus whereon the third dialogue, *i.e.*, the Serissaka Legend proper was engrafted. The story of Pāyāsi's conversion and pious gifts with their heavenly reward seems to have been invented in order just to allay the fear caused in theological circles by atheistical propaganda of the powerful chieftain and philosopher. The tradition of theological defeat and discomfiture at controversy with an atheist like Pāyāsi could not be perpetuated in tact, as it would have been detrimental to the cause of popular religion.

5. Ajita and Pâyâsi:—It may be objected that such theological inventions were unnecessary in a country which is, throughout her history, so remarkable for the freedom of thought, and that Pāyāsi was certainly not the first to promulgate dangerous atheism. Among Buddha's elder contemporaries Ajita was an avowed atheist with a large following. He was an able controversialist, a wandering sophist, held in high esteem by the people of Northern India. If it were necessary to invent mendacious traditions, about the conversion of one atheist, the opponent would say that there would have been similar traditions also about others, while, as a matter of fact, Indian literatures preserve the memory of the atheist Ajita in tact, and hence the supposition of theological invention of pious legends about Pāyāsi, who thought on the lines of Ajita, is untenable. To this our reply is that the analogy does not hold good. In identifying Pāyāsi's case with Ajita's one ought not to forget two facts of great importance: (1) that time had changed since Ajita, and (2) that Pāyāsi, apart from being a philosopher occupied a high social position. While Ajita had flourished in the wake of powerful

sophistic movements and counter movements, destructive of all established religions, Pāyāsi promulgated uncompromising atheism when under the influence of Brahmanism and side by side with the new creeds which arose out of the turmoil of earlier times. Thus Ajita had to combat the custodians of one religious tradition, viz., that of the Brahmins, while Pāyāsi found himself in the midst of other enemies, the theologians of other creeds, the Jainas, the Buddhists and others. Furthermore, Ajita was only a wandering teacher who was virtually out of touch with the common run of people. A sophist like Ajita with his followers might be allowed to hold any set of opinions. His views and actions might not be regarded with so much dread, especially when there were many counterviews and counteractions to avert his influence in the wrong direction. But the case of Pāyāsi was different. The living memory and example of a ruling prince favoured, in spite of his dangerous atheism, with all the riches and honours which fall to the share of mortals would have a totally different effect on the popular mind. The tradition had to be altered so as to enable the theologians to appear before people to their best advantage. But the fact of their defeat at controversy could not at once be concealed; it is echoed in the second dialogue where the chieftain is represented as bestowing gifts, even after his conversion, without faith.

Another legend had to be created to hide, so to speak, this very concealment of facts as well as to avenge the cause of the theologians. The underlying motive of the Serissaka Legend proper was to let people hear from Pāyāsi himself how the neglect of the priesthood is punished in heaven. A similar theological motive seems to have been at work behind the Jaina Upāṅga, Rāya-Paseṇi, which is a dialogue between two controversialists, viz., Pāesi, the king of Seyaviya (Setavya) in Kosala, and the Venerable Kumāra-samaṇa Kesī, a follower of Pārśva. The text belongs to the second stage of the Jaina Canon, and there are internal evidences, such as references to Ceylon, Arabia and Persia[1] which go at once to assign a much later date to the Upāṅga. The classical prose style and the exaggerated novelic descriptions of various vimānas[2] point to the same conclusion. The Jaina account of the controversy[3] is on whole similar to that of the Buddhist, though not identical. Seeing that the two accounts agree in motive and execution, it may not be unreasonable to suspect that the Rāya-Paseṇi has a history of its own; that it is a later recast of an earlier Jaina account now lost. The interest of the Jaina work is that it furnishes a fresh evidence, namely, that the atheistical propaganda

[1] Rāya-Paseṇi ed. Dhanapati, p. 238 :
Simhalihiṃ Âravihim.....Pārasihim.

[2] Ibid, pp. 1-205.

[3] Ibid, pp. 241-296.

of Pāyāsi proved dangerous to all the creeds of the time, Jaina or Buddhist.

6. Date of Serissaka Legend :—Now, if it be granted that the Serissaka legend, or the Sūriyābha-Vimāna story, as the Jaina would say, was engrafted on an earlier tradition of Pāyāsi's conversion and heavenly reward, we have to ask, what is the probable date of the legend proper? Here we have to recall that the earlier tradition was possible only after the death of Kumāra-Kassapa and of Pāyāsi and Uttara. Hence the presumption arises that the date of the legend must have been many years after the deaths of these three personages; but when was it? The controversy itself took place, according to a reliable tradition just after the death of the Buddha. A reasonable interval must also be allowed between the controversy and the three deaths, to which we have to add the years separating the Serissaka legend from the earlier tradition. Prof. Rhys Davids places the date of the Pāyāsi-Suttanta, by modest calculation, within fifty years of Buddha's death.[1]

7. Prose and Poetic versions of Serissaka Legend contrasted :—In the Peta and Vimāna-Vatthu versions of the Serissaka Legend a statement is put into the mouth of Pāyāsi which indicates that the Vīmāna-story came to be composed a hundred years after Pāyāsi's death, but

[1] Dial. B. II. Pt. II.

no statement as to date is to be found in the earlier prose version of the legend in the Pāyāsi-Suttanta. There are so many notable points of difference in the two versions that they could not have been brought about in any very short period. The differences are as follows :—

(*i*) The prose version of the Serissaka Legend is a dialogue between Pāyāsi and Gavampati, the express purpose of which is to bring out in bold relief the distinction between the teacher and the pupil by the difference of heavenly rewards they obtained. The poetic version which occurs in identical form in the "Book of Stories of Heaven and Hell" is on the contrary a dialogue between the angel Pāyāsi and the caravan merchants, which reveals altogether a different purpose, viz., the extolling of virtuous life on earth proceeding from right views of things.

(*ii*) In the prose legend, the god Pāyāsi does not appear to come down to earth; his message is communicated to mankind through the Venerable Gavampati who was a frequent visitor of the Serissaka Ṁansion. In the poetic version, on the other hand, the angel Pāyāsi is represented as conversing on earth with the caravan merchants in distress whom he came down to succour in the midst of a vast sandy desert.

(*iii*) The message of Pāyāsi in the prose version seeks to instruct mankind to cultivate right devotion to the priests, proving by his own existence in the lowest heaven as a lesser reward of pious gifts made without faith, how the gods avenged the cause of theological sectary. In the poetic version, on the contrary, the guardian angel admonishes the distressed merchants in the principles of universal religion.

(*iv*) The prose legend as part and parcel of the Pāyāsi Discourse is clothed in the same dull old fashioned diction of earlier Suttantas, while the narrative in verse is one of the finest specimens of the Buddhist ballads which the Canonical Jātaka Book and the Books of Stories of Heaven and Hell can boast of.

(*v*) Pāyāsi's mansion in the prose version is described as *tuccha* or empty, i.e., lonely, whereas in the Peta and Vimāna anthologies it is characterised as a most magnificent mansion teeming with a retinue of heavenly nymphs and resounding with the symphony of celestial music. This shows that the sharp distinction which was drawn in the prose legend between Pāyāsi and Uttara came to be effaced in course of time.

(*vi*) This inference is well borne out by the fact that in the place of two earlier dialogues we have in the Book of Stories of Heaven two Vimāna-stories, viz., that of Uttara and that of Pāyāsi, describing the glories of each god without implying any invidious distinction.

If we accept the statement of date in the poetic version of the Serissaka Legend, namely, that Pāyāsi met the caravan merchants a hundred years after his death, it follows that the date of the legend in verse cannot be earlier than the Second Council, and considering that Pāyāsi died some years after the Buddha, we must assign to the legend a dàte posterior to the Second Council. Taking other facts into consideration, e.g., the points of difference noticed above, we cannot but conceive a long interval of time, a century or more, between the prose legend and its poetic version.

Judging by the formal and material changes which the Serissaka Vimāna-story underwent, we cannot regard the poetic version of it as a mere prose story versified. If such is not the relation between the two versions of the story, how are we to account for these headlong changes in form and matter? The first thing that strikes us is the introduction of the caravan merchants as interlocutors of Pāyāsi in the poetic version. In the earlier account of the controversy between Kumāra Kassapa and Pāyāsi we come across a parable of caravan merchants, whereby the former tried to persuade the latter to abandon his heresies and there is no dialogue in the Pāyāsi-Suttanta between Pāyāsi and the caravan merchants. This parable, we find, is developed into two stories in the Jātaka-Commentary, viz., the Apaṇṇaka (No. 1) and the Vaṇṇupatha (No. 2). Considering that these Jātakas relate to one birth, they ought to be, according to the earlier principle of enumeration, counted as one Jātaka, and we need not be surprised if they were the outcome of one Birth-story in the earlier collection of 500 Jātakas, i.e., the Canonical Jātaka Book. This supposition presses upon our enquiry concerning the relative position of the Canonical Jātaka Book and the Books of Stories of Heaven and Hell.

8. SERISSAKA LEGEND AFFORDING A COMMON BASIS :—We have seen that strictly speaking the Serissaka-Vimāna-story of the Pāyāsi Discourse in prose was a common historical basis of the poetic version of it, as it occurs in the Peta and the Vimāna Vatthu. It has also been indicated that the poetry

version of the story summarizes on the whole the contents of the Pāyāsi-Suttanta considered as a complete narrative of Pāyāsi. Many Birth-stories, e.g., the Apaṇṇaka, the Vaṇṇupatha, the Litta and the rest developed from the similar legends and parables used as arguments and persuasions by Kumāra Kassapa. Thus it would appear that these Jātakas and the Books of Stories of Heaven and Hell were two parallel growths from the same historical basis, viz, the Pāyāsi Discourse. But looking from another standpoint, i.e., judging from their literary forms and contents, the Peta and Vimāna anthologies may justly be represented as two offshoots of, and developments from the Canonical Jātaka Book. The prose and poetic versions seem to have a direct connection with each other in so far as they seek to inculcate belief in heaven and hell. But the poetic version, as we have noticed, exhibits many new features of its own, which cannot be explained by a theory of direct development. Let us then enquire how these features came to be. These characteristic changes in the poetic version must have a history of their own, and we think that it is the history of the development of the Peta and the Vimāna Vatthu from the Pāyāsi Discourse through a somewhat different literary medium viz. the Canonical Jātaka Book.

9. Jataka a medium for Peta-Vimāna-Stories:—The Peta and the Vimāna Vatthu, as

we now have them, preserve two common stories, viz., the famous Serissaka story and the charming story of Maṭṭakuṇḍalī. The latter occurs in the same ballad form in the Canonical Jātaka Book, as may be judged from the poetical extracts in the Jātaka-Commentary. The occurrence of the story in identical form in the Books of Stories of Heaven and Hell suggests a common source, which appears to us to be the larger anthology of ballads called the Jātaka Book. An objection may be raised that the ballad in the Jātaka Book might have been derived as well from the Peta and the Vimāna Vatthu. We contend that the Books of Stories of Heaven and Hell cannot precede the Canonical Jātaka Book, and our position is defended by the evidence of the Serissaka ballad contrasted with its basis in the prose version as it occurs in the Pāyāsi-Suttanta. The difference of the two versions lies in their morals. While the message of Pāyāsi in the prose version is coloured by theological motive since it teaches mankind to make gifts in faith to the priesthood, the instruction of the angel Pāyāsi in the ballad is free from all theological narrowness, inculcating as it does a religion of universal moral precepts, which is the essential element of the Jātaka-cult. This feature is characteristic of all the ballads in the Peta and the Vimāna Vatthu which have developed a cult which is absent from their basis, the Serissaka Legend in prose, and when we discover that these lesser anthologies are kindred not only in morals, but also in literary forms to the larger anthology, the Jātaka Book, we cannot resist the only legitimate conclusion that the Jātaka Book was the medium through which passed the Serissaka-Vimāna doctrine, and by which *a fortiori* the lesser anthologies were influenced in more ways than one.

Now we will enquire how the Serissaka doctrine promulgating belief in heaven (and hell by implication) could be transmitted through the Jātaka-medium before these ideas of heaven and hell came to be distinctly pronounced in two separate though companion anthologies.

In dealing with the origin of the Jātakas we find that similies or parables were used by the Buddha only as illustrations of certain moral points irrespective of any reference to future existence, while similar illustrations were resorted to by Kumāra Kassapa in his controversy after Buddha's death as arguments in support of his belief in future existence, reward and retribution, expressed in current folk-tales. Kumāra Kassapa utilised the current fables and similes for establishing the popular Law of Karma, implying future existence, reward and retribution, and heaven and hell. At a certain later date the fables used by the Buddha and his disciple Kumāra Kassapa were transformed into Jātakas, or more properly, Suttanta-Jātakas, when a new element, viz., the belief in incarnation crept into them, without losing their original purposes, viz., the inculcation of moral principles and the promulgation of the Law of Karma. Since the popular Law of Karma as expounded by Kumāra Kassapa contributed towards the Jātaka-cult and remained an essential feature of it, we can easily understand how the special Vimāna-doctrine expressed in the Serissaka Legend in prose, viz., belief in heaven, proceeding from the implications of Kumāra Kassapa's arguments, could *a fortiori* flow through the medium of the Jātaka cult.

10. Transformation of prose legend :—But did the earlier Vimāna-doctrine of the Serissaka story in prose leave any trace in course of being transmitted through the Jātaka ? Here, too, we say, Yes. The earlier the Jātaka the more prominent is the trace. All the four Suttantas, which among the earliest forms of Jātakas played a very important role in the development of later Jātaka literatures, viz., the Mahāpadāna, the Mahāsudassana and the rest, bear testimony to a close connection with the Serissaka legend, in language, form, and partly in purpose. The Mahāpadāna Book furnishes instances of communion between man and god, typified respectively by the Buddha and Brahma, while the Mahāsudassana reflects the grandeur of a celestial mansion in the description of kusāvatī, an old idealised city. The Mahāgovinda dazzles the reader's vision

with the sudden illumination which precedes the appearance of the Brahma-mansion, and which acts as a signal for the gods of the Thirty-three assembled in the Sudhammā-Council-Hall to hail the mysterious dweller of the Mansion, Brahmā Sanaṃkumāra alighting to participate in their rejoicings at the surpassing glory of the Buddhist newcomers who have merited abodes in the Tāvatiṃsa Heaven. The Makhādeva relates how Sakka, king of the gods, came down in his chariot the Sudhammā-Hall to escort from the earth, in behalf of the gods of the Thirty-three, the pious king Nimi of Mithilā. And these oldest known Jātakas preserved these traces, even when they were transformed into ballads in the Canonical Jātaka Book, although these traces were eclipsed for a time by the grandeur of poetry, only to reappear in their fullness in the Peta and the Vimāna Vatthu. In other words, the Peta and the Vimāna Vatthu are not selections from the Canonical Jātaka Book, but rather a richer development of the earlier prose legend of Serissaka Mansion under the influence of the Jātaka. The partial independence of the Peta and the Vimāna Vatthu can be substantiated by the fact that these smaller anthologies contain but one story from the Jātaka Book viz. that of Maṭṭakuṇḍalī. Moreover, that they had a common origin is proved by the Serissaka story preserved in identical form in both the Peta and the Vimāna Vatthu,

11. Serissaka ballad in the Petavatthu :—It remains to be explained how the Serissaka Vimāna story could find a place in the Book of Stories of Hell. The only reasonable explanation is that in the earlier Serissaka Legend in prose, there is an idea of punishment implied in the distinction drawn between the heavenly rewards obtained by Pāyāsi and Uttara.The reminiscence of this older distinction is preserved in the two stories of the Vimāna Vatthu, the Uttaravimāna representing Uttara as a dweller of a magnificent abode in the Heaven of the Thirty-three, and the Serissaka-Vimāna representing Pāyāsi as the dweller of a mansion in a lower Heaven, viz., the Cātummahārājika. And it was perhaps to perpetuate the old idea of inferiority that Pāyāsi was made to appear also in the Petavatthu, the main purpose of which was to impress on the people the inevitability of punishment awaiting all wrongdoers in the other world. And since the idea of inferiority in the older Vimāna-doctrine of the prose Serissaka Legend developed into a full-fledged doctrine of Hell, the Vimāna-doctrine must be taken to be prior, at least logically, to the Peta.

12. Chronology of Jātaka and Vimâna Stories :—To sum up, we get the following chronology of the Jātaka and Vimāna stories :—

(*i*) Similes and parables used by the Buddha as illustrations of moral points.

(*ii*) Similes and parables used by Kumāra Kassapa in his controversy, shortly after the death of the Buddha as arguments and persuasions.

(*iii*) The Serissaka Legend in prose in the Pāyāsi-Suttanta, the date of which is placed by Prof. Rhys Davids within 50 years of the Buddha's death.

(*iv*) The Suttanta-Jātakas which can be dated not much later than the Second Council, i.e., a hundred years, more or less, after Buddha's death.

(*v*) The Canonical Jātaka Book, which is earlier than the Vimāna and the Peta Vatthu, the typical Serissaka story of which cannot be assigned, according to tradition, a date exceeding a century after the death of Pāyāsi.

Even if we accept the traditional date of a century, and if we remember that Pāyāsi survived the Buddha, the Serissaka-vimāna story in verse, as it occurs in the Vimāna and the Peta Vatthu, must be assigned a date later than the Second Council, and as we have indicated, this date is later not only than the Suttanta-Jātakas but also than the Canonical Jātaka Book. As to the lower limit of the date of the Serissakavimāna-ballad, and *a fortiori* of the Books of Stories of Heaven and Hell, a conception may be formed in the light of the following evidences.

13. As'oka's Dhamma and Vimâna-Doctrine :—If we analyse Aśoka's religion in the light of his inscriptions with the exception of a few special edicts, we are struck by its close resemblance with the Vimāna-doctrine as we find in the Book of Stories of Heaven, and it is most curious that the special doctrine of the Book of Stories of Hell has not played any part in it. The religion of Aśoka presents two aspects—moral and popular, the former representing a body of moral precepts applicable to all, and the latter comprising faith in the Triad, pilgrimage to holy places to worship the Buddhas, and such public and festive demonstrations as *vimānadasana*, *hastidasana* and illumination (*agikhaṃdhāni*). And these are nothing but the characteristic features of the Vimāna-doctrine above referred to. Whether the Vimānavatthu in its present form existed then or not, it is clear that some Vimāna stories, in some form or other, were known, though not of course in the earlier prose form of the Serissaka story. The phases of belief which have found expression in the Vimānavatthu are characterised by a humanizing spirit rendering the abstract, concrete or practical. The stories teach that the householders can become dwellers of celestial mansions which vary in glory and splendour according to the merits gained by the following acts of piety and religious observances (*dhammacariyā*) :—

(*a*) Faith in the Three Jewels (*tīrataṇesu saddhā*).

(*b*) *Buddhavandanā*—Various modes of salutation to the Buddha, touching his feet (*pādavandanā*) or with folded hands (*añjalikamma*) with a mind transported with joy (*muditamano*), and a heart serene (*pasannacitto.*)

(*c*) *Buddhapūjā*—Worshipping the Buddha with offerings of flowers and perfumes.

(*d*) *Cetiyavandanā*, *Thūpapūjā*, *Dhātu-pūjā*, —Worship of shrines, topes and relics.

(*e*) *Uposatha*—Observance of the Sabbath.

(*f*) *Sīlasamādāna*—Keeping of the precepts.

(*g*) *Kiccāni*—Fulfilment of duties by man and woman.

(*h*) *Āsana*—Cordial reception of the Buddha and his followers.

(*i*) *Dāna*—Liberal gifts of food and drink and other requisites to the Buddha and the Order.

(*j*) *Vihāradāna*—Dedication of *Vihāras* to the Buddha and the Order.

(*k*) *Bhikkhādāna*—Alms-giving.

(*l*) *Ārāma-ropā*, *Vana-ropā*, *Caṅkama*, *Pokkharaṇī*—Laying out of gardens, planting of trees, construction of roads, and excavation of tanks.

(*m*) *Rathapadīpādi*—Gifts of chariots and providing lights, etc.

(*n*) *Puññānumodanā*—Participation in virtuous deeds.

14. Vimāna and Apadāna Stories Contrasted :—These Vimāna ideas of piety were intensified later in the legends of the Apadāna which virtually did away with the precepts and duties of life, and emphasized only such formal aspects of religion as *Pūjā, Vandanā, Dāna and Dakṣiṇā.* Among other differences, the following are the most noticeable :—

1. Like the inscriptions of Aśoka ,the Vimāna stories hold out for the householder a promise of heavenly reward generally in the immediate future,[1] while the Apadāna legends invariably illustrate by the lives of Theras and Therīs how heavenly rewards thus obtained are continued through many cycles of existence and multiplied, until these lead to Arahatship.

2. The Vimānavatthu sets out a religion for the house-holder ,stripped of the idea of renunciation, whereas the Apadāna legends combine by a peculiar mythological device the pious life of the householder with the higher attainments of the recluse, the latter overshadowing the former a synthesis unknown in the time of Aśoka.

3. The Vimāna stories promulgate generally the worship of the present Buddha[2] with his doctrine and followers, while the Apadāna legends by their *Adhikāravāda* exalt the past Buddhas and brings

[1] The Vimāna story of Revatī (No. 52) which also occurs as a Peta-story in the Petavatthu is one of the few exceptions.

[2] The Vimāna story (No. 82) which mentions Sumedha, a past Buddha, is one of the few exceptions.